Impressions of
Jesus

Denis McBride, C.SS.R.

A Redemptorist Publication

By the same author

The Gospel of Luke: A Reflective Commentary
The Gospel of Mark: A Reflective Commentary
Emmaus: The Gracious Visit of God according to Luke
Seasons of the Word: Reflections on the Sunday Readings
The Parables of Jesus
(all available from Redemptorist Publications)

*For my sisters, Ellen and Mary,
and my brother, Patrick,
in love and affection*

Published by
Redemptorist Publications
A Registered Charity Limited by guarantee.
Registered in England 3261721

Photographers:
Cover: The Baptism of Christ by Piero della Francesca
         National Gallery, London
Ron Gregory, pages 6, 26, 70, 84, 100, 138, 168, 206.
David Mansell, page 46.
David Alexander, pages 124, 150, 186, 216.
David Toase, pages 56, 112.

First Printed November 1992
Third Printing June 2000

ISBN 0 85231 137 0

Printed by Zure, Spain

Redemptorist
P U B L I C A T I O N S
Alphonsus House Chawton Hampshire GU34 3HQ
Telephone 01420 88222   Fax 01420 88805
rp@redempt.org   www.redempt.org

Contents

Preface

Our principal resource for understanding the person of Jesus of Nazareth is the four Gospels, yet we know from experience that few of us were introduced to Jesus by a reading of the Gospels. Most of us first learned about Jesus from people who loved him and loved us, people who naturally wanted us to belong to the same community of faith that kept them in contact with the Lord. Christian tradition, for them, was not so much a matter of holding fast to the truth they had been given as handing on the life they had received.

A lively truth of the Christian tradition is that people introduce people to Jesus. And the reason for the introduction is always the same: "so that you may believe that Jesus is the Christ, the Son of God, and that believing this you may have life in his name." (Jn 20:31)

The writers of the Gospels were part of this people-centred process. If none of the evangelists was an eye-witness to the ministry of Jesus, all of them were introduced to the story of Jesus by other people. Each of the evangelists emerged from a different community of people; each of them received and welcomed the message of salvation from earlier generations of preachers and teachers; each of them passed on, in his own creative way, the common tradition he had received. The Church, therefore, gave birth to the Gospels, not vice-versa.

The four evangelists were men of faith who preached the good news through writing. And one of the striking marks of the Gospels is how each of them proclaims the truth about Jesus through showing how his deeds and words affect the people around him. In the beginning there is Jesus, yes; but the Gospels themselves reflect the truth that we best learn about Jesus through those who have a living relationship with him.

It comes as no surprise, therefore, that there is no page or paragraph in the Gospels where Jesus is alone.

When we read the Gospels we meet a litany of individuals and groups who react differently to Jesus and his message. Not only do we learn about Jesus through those who experience new life in him, but also through those who oppose him and reject his message. In exploring such a variety of reactions to Jesus, the evangelists gradually draw us closer to the mystery of their subject and, at the same time, lead us to face our own questions. Where do we stand in relation to all this? Who do we think Jesus is?

This book is an attempt, in a totally different form, to provoke a similar conversation between the reader and Jesus. The impressions that follow are a simple exercise in religious imagination, an attempt to envisage how various people who met Jesus of Nazareth could have reflected on their experience of him. Although the names of some of the characters appear in the Gospels, their stories are not offered as a commentary on the Gospel text. But neither are these stories creations of pure fantasy: they are written out of a faith that attempts to imagine the real in a way that might engage the reader to think again about Jesus.

I would like to thank two Redemptorist confreres, Fr Sean O'Riordan and Fr Beverley Ahearn, for their kindness in reading the text and suggesting improvements, and Sr Myra Cumming, SHCJ, for her tireless work in organising the manuscript for publication. To three people at Redemptorist Publications particular thanks are due: Rosemary Gallagher, my editor, for giving such ready and creative support to the work; Roger Smith, artist in residence, for his design and layout; Rosemarie Pink for her enduring patience in typesetting. Finally, a special word of thanks to the photographers whose own impressions do so much to enliven the text.

A NEIGHBOUR OF JESUS

I come from Nazareth. Someone has to, I suppose. When you come from Nazareth you secretly hope there are duller places in the world, lonely mountain villages where the people are stiff with boredom and the lost sheep are embarrassed to be seen returning home. If there are such places, I would like to know about them – not to go there, of course, but for the assurance that my father and elder brother and myself don't inhabit the most forsaken landscape on God's earth.

I have a suspicion that when God made the world he made Nazareth at the last moment, just after the sun went down. Nazareth is what happens when God works on the sabbath.

Everything about Nazareth is defined by geography. From north to south and from the coast to the Jordan valley, the main trade routes pass us by. We are surrounded by an amphitheatre of hills; but if the setting sounds dramatic, don't be fooled, for there's no great drama unfolding in our midst. Enclosed by brooding stony hills, surrounded by untilled and untillable land, we live in a depression. The scenery could have a stark majesty for a passing stranger, but the hopelessness is native.

Elsewhere there are wheat fields and terraced orchards and vineyards, but not in Nazareth. We huddle in a chalky bowl that is fed by a single spring of water. That water is our solitary natural blessing, our drip of life.

The poor soil and the little water mean that nothing much ever happens here. Most of the men have trades and go to work in Sepphoris, the largest city in Galilee, a few miles north of us. Others work as farm labourers in the estates in the Jezreel valley, just south of us, where my father has a few fields. My father and elder brother have a fierce kinship with the land, taking pride in turning the scraggy ground into a ploughed field where something might grow. They work hard, stooped over the land, delighting in every little sign of growth, feeding each other's mad hope that this year's harvest will yield an abundance. I say nothing. I follow in their wake, a trespasser in their dreams, my eyes fixed on the horizon. Most of the local people put a brave face on everything, but there is little to distract them from the cycle of hardship. There are no surprises, no through traffic, nothing to disturb the awful peace. Few people come here. Sometimes a few hawkers or pedlars will appear, trying to unload what they couldn't sell in Sepphoris, but they rarely tarry long.

There's nothing about Nazareth to attract the outsider; no holy sites where God's word seduced a startled shepherd into becoming a prophet, no ancient places marked by sadness and suffering that might attract the pilgrim of revenge. And if there's nothing about our village to remember, neither is there anything to forget. No glory, no shame. It's as if history has kept a secret promise to pass us by with a distracted air, leaving us famous only by neglect.

I have lived here long enough to know that nothing will ever change. Nothing can. Neither the place nor the people. The whole world seems to be happening behind our backs. Even God seems to have forgotten his little mistake.

The only victory in Nazareth is escape. My favourite pastime is to sit on top of a gully which drops steeply down to the plain of Jezreel and watch the laden caravans head south-east towards Scythopolis, the great city of the Decapolis. I dream of being numbered among those tiny figures heading away from Nazareth, heading towards all sorts of strangers and new experiences.

I love my father, but I don't want to end up like him, stooped from a lifetime's begging from stony ground, tied to a village religion of fear and confinement, not knowing who or what to be angry at.

Someday, I know, I will leave this sad place, just as I know that wherever I go I will always be from Nazareth. When people want to know who we are, they always ask us where we are from. It's as if once people have located us, they can better identify us. Are we more than where we are from? Can a place keep us hostage forever, even when we've shaken the dust from our feet? I'll only know by leaving.

As if to prove me wrong about Nazareth, something did happen last week: Jesus Bar-Joseph came home after an absence of almost a year. I am delighted to see him again, not least because he might bring some life to this dust bowl.

No one was sure why Jesus left. Some people said he went down to Perea to join the revivalist movement of John the Baptist; others claimed he went south to work as a carpenter in one of the big cities and would return to settle down once he had made his fortune. Apart from myself, no one seemed to think that Nazareth itself was a compelling reason for getting away.

His family were hesitant about saying anything definite, as if they didn't want to claim too much. "Time will tell, Joachim," I remember his mother saying to me one day. "We'll have to wait and see."

Whatever the guesswork about Jesus' going, many people regarded his absence as a kind of betrayal. To turn your back on Nazareth is to declare that what you are looking for in life cannot be found here. Leavetaking is always a judgement on those who are left behind. If Jesus' homecoming is an admission that elsewhere is nowhere for a Nazarene to be, he might be forgiven; but I'd be surprised if he has returned as a lost sheep. More like a new shepherd from the look of things.

The whole village now knows that Jesus hasn't come home on a social visit or to settle down again; he has become a travelling preacher and Nazareth is on his schedule. He has come to minister to us. Each evening, after people have finished work and eaten, Jesus can be heard down at the well speaking about the kingdom of God and praying with people. And he hasn't come alone. There are two men with him, who call themselves his disciples. (They have already been nicknamed "the heavyweights".)

Old nosey Martha – our mobile Nazareth Information Centre – is telling everyone that the heavyweights used to be disciples of John the Baptist. They told her, she claims, without her having to ask how they came to know Jesus. "God, I was always fond of Jesus," she confided to me this morning. "I'm not sure about his choice of friends, though. If they leave the Baptist to join Jesus, who knows if they won't leave him too?"

In all the village talk about Jesus, and I've listened to a lot of it, the name of John the Baptist crops up regularly. To account for Jesus' change, people mention John.

Because of John's reputation as a holy man and prophet, many people have sought him out – not only to be baptised, but to ask his advice about what they should do with their lives. By all accounts John is direct, perceptive, critical, encouraging. Many people have changed their lives because of him. Before Jesus went to see John, we all knew him as the son of a local carpenter. Since being with John, Jesus seems to have reinvented himself as a wandering preacher. His identity and direction in life have changed. Not only that, but the other night I heard him speak about John as the greatest man that ever emerged from the womb. Not a casual compliment.

Two of my uncles, who went to hear John two years ago after celebrating Passover in Jerusalem, say that Jesus now sounds like the echo of the Baptist. "Difficult to tell them apart" is their repeated phrase. Now that John has been arrested, this doesn't sound too promising a comparison.

Is John the force behind Jesus' big change? I must confess the question intrigues me. John and his disciples first made their reputation preaching and baptising down in Perea and Judea. They gradually moved north into Samaria, doing the same work around Salim, east of Shechem. About two months ago they moved north again, into Galilee. No sooner had John stepped back into the territory of Herod Antipas than he was arrested, no doubt because his moral authority and popularity posed too great a threat to our nervous tetrarch. Who knows? But answer me this. Is it a coincidence that Jesus started his own ministry immediately after John was arrested? Is it a coincidence that Jesus began where John left off? Why else in the present political climate would Jesus start in Galilee if not to take over from John? Is Jesus our new prophet?

Perhaps some of these questions will be answered in the coming days. Anyway, tomorrow is the sabbath. Tomorrow, I hope, the leader of the synagogue will invite Jesus to read the scriptures and open the word to us.

I arrived at the synagogue earlier than usual, to be sure of a seat, but most of the stools and benches scattered around the meeting place were already taken. The village elders had filled the places in the front row, and they were all staring ahead as if they wanted to distance themselves from the buzz of excitement all around them. Even the regular stragglers were already installed, trying not to look uneasy on seats. Upstairs in the gallery the women were gathering, whispering greetings to one another and settling down to private prayer. I could see old Martha leaning over the gallery as she checked in the arrivals downstairs. I felt a kinship with her somehow: like myself, she welcomes every distraction during these long services. But not this sabbath. Nobody would be easily distracted from the main business. The whole village was out in force to listen to the local prophet.

From the middle of the synagogue I saw my father stand and signal to me that there was a place beside him, and when I squeezed in between him and my brother I could see Jesus two benches in front of us. He was fingering the tassels of his prayer shawl.

"He must be nervous," I whispered to my brother.

"Who?"

"Jesus, of course."

"Then say a prayer for him," he said.

I closed my eyes and said a quick one, asking God to give Jesus strength to face his own crowd.

When I opened my eyes I saw the hazzan – who acts as the synagogue's caretaker and master of ceremonies and primary school teacher – begin to move around the hall sprinkling an infusion of mint on the floor, to purify the air. With so many people crowded into the hall, there wasn't much floor space left to sprinkle. I said another quick prayer, this time that the mint would do its job.

At last the time came to begin. The hazzan invited us to stand and face Jerusalem. A reader walked up to the platform and began to recite the Shema Israel. His voice was clear in the gathered hush: "Hear, O Israel: there is no Lord but the Lord our God, and you shall love the Lord your God with the love of your whole heart, and your whole soul, and your whole strength...." At the end of the call to observance, we all added our Amen. Next came the long surge of the Shemoneh Esreh, calling on us to glorify the Almighty, the God of Abraham, of Isaac, of Jacob, the great Master who gives all good things, the great Being from whom all wisdom and holiness proceeds. After each benediction, we again announced our Amen.

After the prayers were said, the assembly sat down again. Throats were cleared, veils and prayer shawls adjusted, phylacteries confirmed in place. One of Jesus' disciples leaned over and whispered something in his master's ear, but I couldn't tell if Jesus responded.

The hazzan moved from his place behind the reader's platform and walked slowly towards what we as children called "the secret place." He pulled aside the long, red curtain and I could see the flames of the lamps glowing in the dark, windowless space. The lamps lit up the tebah, the sacred cupboard where the scrolls of the Law and the Prophets are kept, together with the horns and trumpets that are sounded on days of fast and feast. After opening the tebah, the old man lifted out the ancient leather case and unwound the ties around it. It seemed an age before he unwrapped the linen cloths protecting the scrolls and selected a scroll of the Law. He carried it to the base of the platform, unrolled it, then handed it to the leader of the synagogue.

I'm sure I caught a sigh of disappointment from the assembly as Lamech climbed the three steps of the platform to read. The selected passage was taken from one of Moses' speeches, read first in Hebrew and then in Aramaic:

The Lord your God will raise up for you a prophet like myself, from among yourselves, from your own brothers; to him you must listen...

You may say in your heart, "How are we to know what word was not spoken by the Lord?" When a prophet speaks in the name of the Lord and the thing does not happen and the word is not fulfilled, then it has not been spoken by the Lord. The prophet has spoken with presumption. You have nothing to fear from him.

The leader of the synagogue rolled up the scroll and handed it back to the hazzan. He looked out at the waiting assembly. We looked back.

"We are a people of expectation," he said. "Our history has educated us to wait in hope, to look to the fulfilment of the words of Moses. Those sacred words hold a promise and a warning. One day, Moses says, a prophet like himself will emerge from our midst. That prophet, whom we call *the Prophet,* is the promise. Many others will come speaking empty words. That is the warning.

"The Prophet we await will be like Moses. Like Moses. That is how we will recognise him. Who was Moses? Among men he was Ish Eloakhim, the Man of God. Among prophets he was a colossus. Among Jews he is both miracle and paradox. We don't know where he came from. Egypt, not Israel, dominated his life. It was there he was smuggled as an infant, educated as a prince, forced to flee as a murderer, commanded to return as a protester, empowered to leave as a liberator.

"Moses was God's masterpiece and God's victim, the stranger destined to belong nowhere but the heart of God. He was the first man to hear the name of God, the only prophet to speak mouth to mouth with the Almighty, the one creature to see God face to face. Of all men he was God's intimate on earth, the one who received the Law, the sacred Torah, on the Mountain of God. It was he who led our people through hunger and terror and wilderness to the gates of the Promised Land. Humility was his stance before God; fidelity was his preoccupation; unyielding loyalty to the Torah was his gift to us. His story is our past; his word is our future. He is the candle in the dark of history.

"Without Moses, who would we be? I don't know. But this I do know: after Moses, history was never the same again. Because of him we look to the Prophet, the one who will surely free us from the yoke of the new Pharaoh. When the Prophet appears, we will know him. How could we miss such a giant in our midst?

"While we wait for him, we have nothing to fear from prophets who trade in empty words and lead people forever into wilderness. The only thing we have to fear is our desperation. So fervently do we long to look on the face of the Prophet that we are in danger of making some holy innocent into someone he is not destined to be. We must guard against our hunger for immediacy. We can make a golden calf, or a wooden prophet, or a stone idol; but only the Almighty can create a human masterpiece, only the God of our forefathers can anoint another Moses.

"No, we must not cheat ourselves. We must look

within. Moses belongs not only to history but to the landscape within us, the greatness we carry in our hearts. Out of this greatness, not out of our desperation, will we recognise the Prophet. Until the day of his coming, we wait in the hope that is rooted in God's word. God will call the new Moses out of Egypt. And when he does appear, my dear people, you will have no need to ask me if he is the one."

When he had finished commenting on the reading, the leader of the synagogue stayed for a few moments on the platform. He looked around the assembly as if he were incuriously eyeing a group of seated strangers. I thought he was thinking of saying more, but he looked tired and drained, like a man who had no words left in him. The hazzan moved forward and helped him down off the platform, and he returned to his place among the elders.

"Well spoken, Lamech!" shouted someone from behind me.

"A word for our time!" someone else cried.

From all around the synagogue came murmurs of approval; people were nodding their heads in agreement; some turned to their neighbours to share a few words.

"Surprised the old man has so much life in him," my brother whispered to me. "Not bad, not bad at all."

When the talking had died down, the hazzan called the meeting to prayer. We stood up and a new reader led us in a litany of praise to God and thanksgiving for his Law. As the prayers were coming to a close the hazzan returned to the tebah where he unwrapped one of the scrolls of the Prophets, for the second reading. Holding the scroll in both hands, he returned to the base of the platform just as the prayers were concluded. We all sat down.

Jesus remained standing. It's going to happen, I thought,

and I hope to God it happens well. Jesus eased himself past his disciples and walked up to the front. The hazzan handed him the scroll. Jesus smiled his acknowledgement and ascended the platform. All eyes in the synagogue were fixed on him. Unrolling the scroll he quickly found the passage he had chosen to read, words of the prophet Isaiah. These he proclaimed:

The Spirit of the Lord is upon me,
because he has anointed me to preach good news to the poor.
He has sent me to proclaim release to the captives
and recovering of sight to the blind,
to set at liberty those who are oppressed,
to proclaim the acceptable year of the Lord.

He rolled up the scroll and handed it back to the hazzan. We waited, like the captive audience we were. Was he going to preach? or was he just recalling how the holy prophet gave hope to the poor and the oppressed in exile in Babylon? Or what?

Jesus continued, "Today this scripture has been fulfilled in your hearing."

We waited for more, but nothing more was said. There was to be no sizing up his opponents, no graceful introduction, none of the usual rhetoric of preaching. Just one blast of the trumpet. That was it!

Have you ever heard a sermon of one line? Have you ever heard a sermon claim so much by saying so little? If what was said was true, it was more than enough. As it turned out, it was too much.

When Jesus said no more, at first his silence forced people to think about what he had said. The leader of the synagogue had counselled all of us to wait in expectation. Jesus was announcing that the time of expectation was over, that ancient prophecy was being fulfilled, not just recalled, in the synagogue in Nazareth. In our hearing. (This, I thought, will be the first time anything has ever been fulfilled in Nazareth.)

People were surprised at the way he spoke, with authority and assurance; some may even have been impressed; but with nothing more being said, everyone's attention was drawn back to the figure that still stood on the platform. Jesus looked vulnerable, unimpressive, a bit lost – not the kind of new Moses you'd expect to usher in the today of ancient prophecy. From all around me I could hear voices gradually fill the silence. If people were unsure about what Jesus said, they were certain who Jesus was; and they weren't going to allow scripture to interfere with their memories of him. I could hear some of the exchanges.

"Who does he think he is?"

"You'd think he was talking to strangers."

"The nerve of the man, standing up there claiming to be the Lord's anointed. What are we supposed to do? Clap?"

"If there's one thing I hate, it's people trying to be someone they're not."

"His mother and brothers and sisters are right here in the synagogue. They must be embarrassed out of their minds."

"His family should do something about him."

"He's nuts, I tell you. We've got ourselves a new village idiot."

"He's no idiot. He's just trying his luck."

"A chancer, if ever I saw one. Just like our Joshua."

"He might get away with this kind of talk down south, but he can't fool us. No, sir."

"Who does he take us for? Idiots?"

"I never thought I'd see the day when one of my own

family would lose his head in public. We'll never live this down."

"The poor devil isn't responsible. The wilderness must have got to him."

"Mark my words, no good can come from all this. No good at all."

As the chorus of disapproval gained momentum, some people rose from their seats and started shouting up at the platform. The mood was becoming ugly; it was as if something else had entered the synagogue. The hazzan was signalling to Jesus to leave the platform, but Jesus stood facing the aggression like he was determined to get used to it.

"Who do you think you are? Moses?" someone shouted.

"Prove to us you're a prophet. Bet you didn't see this coming!"

"Come off it, Jesus! You know us and we know you! Let's not pretend! You can't fool your own crowd!"

"Stick to carpentry, sonny boy, and leave religion to the experts."

My view of the platform was suddenly blocked when Raban the builder rose to his full height in front of me, shouting "Impostor!" He picked up the stool he'd been sitting on and started brandishing it in the air. He looked angry enough to throw it. I became afraid of what I couldn't see, so I stood up to see around him.

At this point the hazzan was mounting the steps of the platform, and when the crowds saw him they greeted his appearance with a cheer. Officialdom had arrived. In a strange way the old man looked as if he had grown much older between the Law and the Prophets. Nothing like this ugly circus had ever happened in his long years of service, and he seemed unsure and frightened. He held up his hands for silence, then said something to Jesus.

Jesus nodded his head, but instead of leaving the platform, he turned again to face us all. He looked defiant, a man among his own about to cancel everything behind him, a lover about to take leave of those he could not keep.

He shouted out, "Hate solves nothing! A prophet is only despised in his own country, among his own relations and in his own house!"

At this accusation, all hell seemed to break loose. I couldn't see much because by now the whole synagogue was on its feet, shouting and screaming. The air was bursting with abuse. It was if years of reserve and frustration and anger, about whatever, exploded into a village riot. Nazareth had someone to blame at last for all the misery, and nobody was going to lose out.

I pushed forward to where the two disciples were standing. They looked like they were waiting for the heavens to open.

"Get Jesus out of here!" I shouted at them.

They continued standing where they were.

"Do it now!" I screamed. "Go, before they split his skull open!"

I shoved them forward, and only then did they start pushing their way to the front. As they elbowed and shouldered people out of their way, they looked more like the heavyweights they were supposed to be. I stood on tiptoe, craning for a view of the platform, but I could only see backs and heads.

I jumped up on a bench. The platform was empty, but around the base there was a knot of people clustered about Jesus. One of the elders, his face flushed with anger, was prodding Jesus in the chest with his forefinger as he made his objections felt. Others pushed Jesus from behind. After what seemed an age, the disciples broke through the group, grabbed Jesus by the arms, pulled him in between them and started pushing their way back down the synagogue, towards the doors.

Two or three people started a chant, which was taken up by the crowd: "Get lost, get lost, get lost!" All around the synagogue people were stamping their feet and clapping their hands. The roar of rejection was deafening.

As the two disciples hustled Jesus past where I was standing, I jumped down from the bench and followed in their wake, to get out of the madhouse. Just as we got to the doors, a terrible high-pitched scream broke from somewhere in the gallery. It cut through the manic chanting and rose above the pounding rhythm of the clapping and stamping. As Jesus and the disciples ran from the synagogue, the woman's piercing cry seemed to get louder and longer. It sounded as if it would never stop, as if nothing could outstay its guttural pain, as if it would hang in the air forever.

Jesus has gone. The last I saw of him was from the doorway of the synagogue – a runaway prophet disappearing in a cloud of dust. He was lucky to get away. I'm sure it was the first of many emergency exits, just as I'm sure the day will come when he'll run out of luck.

Nazareth will recover from its brief violent affair with Jesus, but I doubt if Jesus will get over the hurt so easily. He must be sore with disappointment. Whatever Jesus hoped to find in Nazareth isn't there. Whatever expectations brought him back must now be well dead. I'd be surprised if he ever returns. Why should he? More to the point, how can he?

I still feel saddened by the whole shabby business, and angry that Jesus has been rejected so quickly and finally. This morning I went over to see old Martha, as I always do when I want to talk. She's always there when I need her.

"What are you so surprised about?" she asked. "For most of us here, Nazareth is the centre of the world, Nazareth is the way things are."

"What has that to do with anything?"

"Look around you, Joachim, look around you. Nazareth explains itself. The houses are the same, the streets are the same, the people are the same. There's no room here for local heroes. Jesus will be fine somewhere else."

"Am I the only one who wanted him to stay?"

"You're young. You want change. You're our village fidget. You're open to the mad possibility that a prophet might emerge from this outback. Most of us find that too much to take. For all our complaints and moans about the place, we don't really want things to change. That's not a crime."

"It's death, Martha."

"It's the only life we know. Don't get mad at the people here. We're not stupid or perverse or vicious. We're just ordinary folk leading ordinary lives. Jesus was asking too much, expecting too much from those who know him. We've all got memories, and we can only see in him what we've always seen in him. No more, no less. That's all we know. Maybe that's all we can take."

"I can't take it for much longer," I said. "I'm getting out."

Martha looked at me without saying anything. She started to nod her head slowly, perhaps to confirm what she had suspected for a long time. She raised her hand as if she were about to make some point, but lowered it again to her side.

Her unusual silence made me feel slightly awkward. She moved over to a small table by the window, picked up a cloth and wiped her eyes, her face, her neck. If she knew I was longing for her response to what I said, she gave no hint of it. She stood looking out the window for a long time, her hands flat on the table in front of her; it seemed as if something way up on the hill had captured her complete attention. I sat behind her, in the grey-dark coolness of the room, looking at her head outlined in the window. I could hear sounds coming from outside, like the soft patter of receding steps.

When she spoke at last, her voice had a desperate sureness about it. "Get out of here while you can, Joachim. You're young and healthy – there's nothing to keep you here, nothing to hold you back. Follow your star wherever it may lead you. And when you go, stay away for a long time. Don't be rushing back."

"Why do you say that?"

She did not move from her position at the window, but kept her attention fixed on something outside.

"Don't be offended, Joachim. I'm saying this because I love you like the son I never had. You know I'll miss you when you go."

"But why shouldn't I come back soon?" I insisted.

"What for? If you return too soon you won't find whatever drew you back. You'll find what Jesus found – your place gone, your traces covered. People will have changed just at the time you want them to be the same as before. Stay away until you have carved out your own place in the world, until you no longer expect anything of Nazareth, until you have no need to press yourself on those you left behind. Then when you come back, you might be grateful to this barren land, you might see more in these stubborn people, you might even be free to love this place of your birth."

She turned away from the window and faced me. At

that moment I thought she looked like a secret saint, refined by years of confinement and suffering, who had hidden her real self behind the mask of a village gossip. I stood up. She looked at me with those huge moist eyes as if all her hopes were concentrated in what I would do with my life.

"Are you listening to me, son?" she asked.

She came over to me, put her arm around my shoulder and pulled me in to her generous warmth, as she always did when it was time for me to go.

"Yes, Martha, I'm listening," I said. "I'm listening real good."

THE WOMAN OF SAMARIA

I have become a stranger to this early morning ritual of gathering at the town well. For the first time in years, I've come here in the hope of finding my place amidst the scatter of buckets and pitchers and waiting women. When I arrive, the talk dies down. I look around. I know almost everyone, and everyone, no doubt, knows of me. I feel a real gawk. A few of the women look at me, smile a greeting, and look away again. It's difficult to interpret their smiles – whether terminal or just awkward. Others raise their heads as though they might look, but they seem to think better of it and keep their eyes fixed on the empty vessels in front of them as if they're schooling themselves in solemnity. I close my eyes for a moment and tighten my grip on the new buckets I'm carrying.

"Well, well, well!" someone shouts. "Look who we have here! Diana the huntress herself! There are no wild boars here, my dear!"

Nobody laughs, nobody takes up the insult I know I deserve. What can I say?

From somewhere on my left I hear a voice calling my name. A hand reaches out and pulls me into a small group near where I'm standing. "Welcome back," a voice says. It's Julia, who in the old days used to see me as a rival for her husband's affections. I'm so grateful to her now that

I drop my buckets and embrace her. Her hair smells of cinnamon. She giggles nervously, but looks pleased with herself for her brave kindness. The three other women stop fidgeting and, one by one, repeat Julia's greeting. As I nod my thanks I hope I don't look too stupid in my relief.

None of them makes a fuss, no one starts to probe. Gradually they draw me into the easy flow of their talk. Somehow they manage to give the impression of continuing a conversation broken off only yesterday. I know they must wonder how I managed to get through so many days and nights since they last spoke to me, but they keep their curiosity in check.

Miriam, my youngest niece, joins our group and nods shyly in my direction as she hugs herself; I feel her arrival like a touch of blessing. Will the rest of the family, even though they know the old stories, meet me as readily?

As the talk continues I discover how easy it becomes to slip into simple words and gestures, and the hope of renewed friendship that I thought dead forever comes to life again. But even as it happens I wonder if it will last. When Jesus leaves our town tomorrow, will people still make moves to accept me?

We squat, we exchange a little news, we engage in the lively superficiality of everyday existence while we await the arrival of the town water-master, whose responsibility it is to unlock the cover of the well for a brief time each morning. Miriam finds her voice and explains to me that he has become frail and forgetful these last few years, and that sometimes she has to go and seek him out. Listening to her now I wonder if she knows how I have watched her through the grille of my window, have heard her calling his name, and have longed for her to call on me.

"Here he comes!" someone shouts.

There is a scramble for buckets and pitchers. I watch Miriam watching the old man picking his way through a caravan of traders arriving in the market-place. When he bumps into a heavily laden donkey and is roundly cursed by its owner, she edges forward a few paces. He pauses for a moment to rub his bruised side and check his keys are secure in his belt. Miriam glances back in my direction and then goes over to meet him. I see his face become a smile; I see her leaning over to whisper some special greeting in his ear.

I start praying inside that this venerable elder will not dismiss me as he did before, on the command of the town council. When he approaches the well, the talk dies away. Everyone waits to see what will happen. He shuffles towards us and stops in front of me, a key in his right hand, a stick in his left.

Without a word he offers me his right hand, then signals with his stick for me to open the well.

The day after I left my husband was the day I was told never to use the town well again. I was a pollutant; that was official. The prohibition was equivalent to banishing me, but I refused to be driven out of my own town, even though I knew I had no remedy in law and could not divorce my husband.

He was a cloth merchant whose job involved a great deal of travelling. He soon earned enough to build a large house, which faced across the market-place to the well. His house stood as a public testament to his success and often visitors would pause to admire its difference, sometimes inquiring if a Roman official lived there. My husband was easily pleased when he heard about this.

When he returned home from his travels, he was always exhausted. In the early days of our marriage he would make me laugh with stories about faraway places and strange people; but the stories, like the laughter, began to run out as time passed. I can't remember when things started changing for the worse. We didn't have a big fight, there was no showdown, there was no particular time you could point to and say: That's when it all started. One day you just find yourself saying as I did: "What's happening to us? Tell me. We started out as good people and look at us now. We can't look at one another, we can't talk to one another."

I began to feel uncomfortable because I wasn't used to being around people who would suddenly go quiet. I began to wonder what I'd done wrong. I came from a family of talkers, and one of the things that attracted me to my husband was his easy ability to communicate. He was a good talker, language was part of his trade; but after a few years of marriage he grew into the quiet man of Shechem when he came home. He would brighten up when friends came for dinner, but as soon as they left it was as if he had used up his attention for that day and had to start saving up again.

The times I pressed him to talk to me he would always start boasting about how his amorous ways had succeeded with Roman women. He was an easy-going conqueror, apparently. Meanwhile, my role was to play his compliant and indulgent wife, smiling at his playful follies, attentive to the welfare of the one who had spared me the humiliation of being left unclaimed. I was supposed to be content making togas for Roman husbands – who were his best clients – while my own unrequited passion was somehow to be subsumed into holy resignation

After nine years, I became tired of his reality and his togas.

One morning I told him that I would be out of his life

by evening. I had finally reached the stage where I couldn't take any more. I had already arranged to move in with an old maid who lived on the outskirts of the town; although her house was only one room, I knew that there I would be free of him at last. He didn't shout or scream or weep when I told him, but warned me that I would end up lonely and loony and would surely be disgraced for the rest of my life. When he started quoting Jewish scripture at me, I guessed the depth of his desperation. The words he used come from the wisdom writing of someone called Jesus son of Sirach. My husband turned them into a curse, and I remember them as a prisoner remembers the bites of a lash:

> I would sooner keep house with a lion or a dragon
> than keep house with a spiteful wife.
> Like a thirsty traveller she will open her mouth
> and drink any water she comes across;
> she will sit down in front of every tent-peg
> and open her quiver to any arrow.

That was venom dressed up as wisdom. I told my husband he could peddle his wares and his sanctimonious masculine quotations somewhere else. And I did not wait for evening to be rid of him.

After I left, I puzzled over the question why it had taken me so long to leave my husband. Why are we so hesitant to leave what we know isn't working? What is this curious compulsion to stay with a disaster we know will go on and on and on? Why do we co-operate in our own defeat when we know nothing will ever change? Really change, I mean.

How mean are the lives we live, enclosed by our own limitations, confined by our failure to imagine things could be different. What passes as dignified perseverance is often only cowardice, a gutless decision to stay in place. Sometimes we dream of packing our bags and making for the bridge, but our dream never finds us actually crossing. We set up our tent on the bridge. We falter, we watch the traffic heading elsewhere, we tarry too long. We look back like the Israelites in the desert and wonder if the security that went with bondage is preferable to the pain that goes with freedom. Unlike them, we find ourselves slinking back to our old haunts, under cover of darkness. And then we drink to our wise decision, consoling ourselves that we have no right of way in any other future. So, it's business as usual, back to decorating our tombs with cosy furniture, back to the place where nothing changes. The future has to happen somewhere else.

I trusted my husband as I trusted in the future of our marriage. All those years I served him faithfully, I believed I was doing the right thing. It was important for me to honour the choices I had made, even though I came to suspect that life had somehow passed me by. That, as you might know, can be a paralysing experience.

Have you ever had the experience of friends passing you by in the street, leaving you looking in puzzlement after them as you try to work out what you've done wrong? It isn't that they are wilfully ignoring you; they are altogether distracted, intent on being somewhere else. Life can be like that.

Many times I've wondered what it might have been like if I had led a different life, attached myself to someone who would have cared for me as I would have cared for him. But dwelling on what might have been only sharpened the pain of the present moment. I tried to discipline myself to be grateful for the life I did have.

I used to spend hours trying to make a list of things I

should be grateful for, moments that might redeem the sense of loss I felt so keenly. But when you wake to the real mess you've been covering up in your life, you begin to suspect the past. It's as if you can't be sure any more what really happened in the past. It hits you that you might have misread everything. Which is why the effort of trying to recall good times, reimagining the past to prop up the present, wearied me beyond telling. I ran out of fiction.

The point was this: if I stayed with my husband, I knew we would never get to the point when things could be different. Never. That realisation had an ally within me, a growing restlessness that couldn't be sedated. These two things together gave me courage to pack my bags and move on.

Far out beyond the last house in the town, past where the oaks and the terebinths stand in huge clumps, there is an ancient well that is used only by passing travellers and shepherds. It is known as Jacob's well. Although its curved walls go deep into the earth, the water is never plentiful; indeed, sometimes I managed to draw out only half a bucketful. But that was enough to survive on. It had to be.

I trekked out there each day for years, on my own. Sometimes, I admit, I didn't return alone. Ever since the old woman died, the well became a presence in my life, and with each waking morning its importance grew. It became my only sure destination, my only source of water, the only place I could meet people who weren't troubled by my past. Some of the characters I met there were rough and curt, some strived too anxiously to taste my hospitality. With a few, however, I was able to satisfy my need for human company. And when they took their leave, as they always did, I would lie in bed alone at night knowing that the well would be there in the morning, waiting for me as usual.

On my way out to the well yesterday, I passed several men on their way into town. They were Jews and they gave me a wide berth. The sound of their voices rang out impatiently as I passed, arguing about "places of honour" in some kingdom. From their accents I could tell they were Galileans; from the looks of them they didn't appear to be the kind of people who'd have much cause to worry about their celebrity status – least of all where they were heading. Good luck to them, I thought, as I adjusted the bucket on my head and slapped another mosquito off my face.

I was thirsty.

It was only when I came up to the well that I noticed a man sitting on the far side, on the ground, his chin resting on his knees, his arms clasped around his legs. He was alone. I wondered if he was waiting for someone. I put my bucket on the ledge and pulled the rope towards me. I glanced down at the man. Not a move. Asleep, I thought. I tied the rope onto the handle of the bucket.

"I'm thirsty" a voice said. "Give me something to drink."

Not asleep, I thought. The man had to be talking to me, although his back was still towards me. He didn't move. Whoever he was, he was a bit short on charming introductions. Another Galilean, judging by his accent; just another man, judging by his presumption that others should jump to answer his needs. I waited to see the shock on his face when he turned around to see who it was he was addressing. But he stayed put.

I lowered the bucket, easing the rope through my fingers. I'd give him the bucket all right, I thought.

"You are a Jew," I said.

"I am," he said. He rose and turned to face me. I looked at him. No shock.

"I am a Samaritan."

"I know," he said.

"You are a man."

"Indeed I am," he said.

"I am a woman."

"I can see that," he said.

"Then why are you asking me for a drink?"

"Because I'm thirsty," he said. "Thirst brings us all to the well."

So much for trying to put him in his place, I thought. He seemed more polite than at first. Besides, I hadn't spoken to a soul in five days, not since my latest live-in companion had flown the nest. And in my position you couldn't afford to be too choosy.

I pulled the bucket out of the depths and untied it from the rope, aware that all the time he was watching me. The bucket was lighter than usual, almost empty. There was hardly enough water to satisfy anyone's thirst. Still, I offered what there was to him, thinking his need was probably greater than mine. He smiled his gratitude, cupped his hands, dipped them into the bucket, and bringing the water to his mouth he drank it slowly, as if he were a guest of honour savouring the choice wine at a banquet.

When he had finished drinking, I looked into the bucket. It was empty. As I tied it onto the rope to lower it again, he said:

If only you knew the gift of God,
and who it was who is saying to you,
'Give me a drink,'
you would have asked him,
and he would have given you living water.

I know I'm a wee bit slow, but it seemed puzzling to me how a man can empty your bucket and then offer you water. Maybe this was his line with women, I thought.

I reminded him that he didn't have a bucket and asked him how he meant to get this water. Who did he think he was, anyway? Our father Jacob, son of Isaac, son of Abraham, gave us this well. Jacob I knew. Jacob was the one who arrived in life too late, but who made up for it by lying to his father, cheating his twin brother out of his inheritance, and deceiving his father-in-law. Jacob was the first great dreamer, who dreamed of a ladder he couldn't climb. Jacob was the fugitive who had to run away from home to find a wife, and was lucky to find the beautiful Rachel at a well on the reaches of the wilderness. Jacob was the dedicated romantic, who worked for seven years to marry his beloved Rachel, but was tricked into marrying her elder sister. Jacob was the one who married Rachel a week later, but was then made to work seven more years for a thug of a father-in-law. Jacob was the great lover who had two wives and two concubines, who, between them, gave him warm nights and a tribe of children. Jacob was the shy warrior who wrestled in the dark with a mysterious stranger at the ford of Jabbok. Jacob was the wounded one who refused to let his assailant go before being blessed by him. Jacob was the one whose name was changed to Israel because he showed his strength against God and prevailed. Jacob was the repentant one who, even though he wrestled the Almighty without a tear, bowed down seven times before the brother he had cheated, called him Lord, and wept. Jacob was the great provider who died in exile in Egypt; but before he died, he gave his beloved son, Joseph, a special gift: he gave him Shechem. Jacob is the only great figure the Bible calls *ish tam,* the plain, quiet man, the one who never resorted to violence. Jacob, our ancestor, I know him, I honour him, I love him.

But who was this stranger at Jacob's well? Who was this man who wanted me to ask him for a drink? No doubt this Mr Fixit was greater than Jacob and could divine water anywhere.

He didn't get angry at my remarks. That surprised me. Nor did he dismiss me as an upstart Samaritan. That surprised me even more. He said:

> Whoever drinks this water
> will get thirsty again;
> but those who drink the water I shall give
> will never be thirsty again:
> the water I shall give
> will turn into a spring inside them,
> welling up to eternal life.

I didn't understand what he was saying but I was intrigued by his determination to say it. If he knew a source of water that would save me the bother of trekking out here, then it would be useful to know where it was. But would I meet anyone at his secret well? What would be the point of drinking deeply if I had to drink alone? People thirsted for more than water. Surely he knew that.

He told me to sit down, then he sat beside me on the stone ledge of the well. We must have looked a rare sight, I tell you: two mismatched souls sitting at a well in the hot sun, looking out at the mountains where Adam and Eve made their false start, and where Noah offered worship after the flood. We were surrounded by the geography of misery and mercy.

My pious reflection was interrupted by his question: "Why don't you go and call your husband, and come back here?"

"I don't have a husband," I replied. "I'm a free woman."

"How many lovers have you had? Five, six?"

The question seemed to have erupted from the well, but it must have come from him.

"You've got bucketfuls of gall!" I barked at him. "What on God's earth gives you the right to ask questions like that? Are you some kind of weirdo who hangs around wells until you can get some defenceless woman to brighten your day with the details of her sex life? What is it with you?"

"I'm sorry you're hurt," he said.

"Sorry I'm hurt, are you? Where have I heard that before? No doubt you'll say next that this hurts you more than it hurts me."

"Not if you don't want me to," he said.

"Do us both a favour and go away," I said. "Goodbye, water salesman, goodbye."

He was supposed to get up, turn his back on me, walk away to wherever he was supposed to be going, and leave me in peace. But he didn't move. Stubborn, I thought, this man is seriously stubborn.

What a question to ask anyone! How many lovers? When you've been abandoned by a succession of lovers, it's not the arithmetic that kills you, is it? Yes, I've been approached, charmed, lured, prevailed upon, used, measured up, found wanting, left behind. But I've been a willing victim to this predictable passion story, as if I were randy for disappointment. You'll have guessed by now that I've never learned from my failures or outgrown my mistakes. Memory is a useless teacher for addicts like me. I am a veteran loser.

Lover, loser. Only time spells the difference.

Perhaps that's why my lovers have always left me so quickly, always while they thought I was asleep, tiptoeing out of my life to escape from the odour of defeat. At least

I've been spared the humiliation of having to listen in the daylight to a man with itchy feet rehearse his tactics of withdrawal, thinking he could cover his going with words. What are words without promises? What the hell good are words when you've got nothing else in your life but their insufferable echo?

The trouble with the man sitting beside me, I thought, is that he doesn't know when to get lost. He started to say something, then faltered. When he did speak, I could tell by his tone that he was nervous of another scalding from me.

"I know you're angry with me for what I said. Sometimes I wonder if I have a curious gift for upsetting people."

"No need to wonder for long on that one," I said.

He laughed. "You're right," he said. He bent down and started to adjust the strap on one of his sandals. It didn't look to me like it needed any adjusting. Nervousness, I thought, as I watched a small grey lizard scurry into hiding at the edge of a boulder and try to teach itself to look like a stone. There's survival, I thought, perfect blending.

My companion in thirst cleared his throat and turned towards me. "Believe me when I tell you that no one who drinks the water I can give need ever be thirsty again. You know in your heart that this well is no place to quench your thirst, and you have a great thirst. Time and time again you come out here hoping to find what you long for, and time and time again you draw out fresh disappointment. Yet you still come, hoping to meet your Jacob. You go back with your fresh water and your new man, and when you discover how quickly they run out on you, you return here hoping for more. In all these years you've never lost the habit of hoping or your desire to be satisfied. But this well is not the answer. It can't be."

The white-hot sun was beating down on both of us, and my thirst was growing into an ache inside me. I looked for my lizard, but he had gone to stone somewhere else. Whoever this man was, I knew he was more than a thirsty traveller. Were my needs so easily read by strangers? Was this man a prophet? I looked at his face and wondered what lay behind those troubled, knowing eyes. Had he any idea what it was like being regarded as a freak by your own people? Did he know what suffering could spring from leaving and being left, from belonging to no one, from being told that you don't fit into anyone's scheme for the future? Was he aware that it was desperation, not hope, that drove me out to this hunting ground?

At this point, I thought I'd raise the tone of the conversation a little, so I asked my Jewish prophet if the proper place to worship was on the Samaritan Mount Gerizim or in the Jewish Temple in Jerusalem. I admit, in case you have any doubts, that this was not an agonising question for me; but it would, I thought, serve to move the conversation away from too much probing into my sad, ridiculous sex life. Liturgical discussions have their uses. But I wanted also to test him, to find out if his religion would get the better of him, to see whether it was curiosity or compassion that kept him beside me.

But he wasn't interested in liturgical mountaineering or in rehearsing old quarrels. What's the point of worshipping God, he wondered, if we cannot bring ourselves to what we're doing? The name of the Father, he insisted, can only be hallowed in the spirit of truth.

Back to truth, I thought, back to me facing the truth about myself. I wasn't sure what he meant about worship, but I was sure he wasn't budging. It was then I decided to risk telling him my story. Why then? Why at all?

Maybe it was because I felt that he, unlike other men I'd met, would not be frightened by real storytelling. I don't know. Why do any of us open up to strangers? Why do we confess things to people we meet by chance? You tell me.

I told him how sometimes I saw the well as a deep, dark enclosure full of stale smells and the echoes of dropped promises. At other times, I admitted, the depths yielded up some refreshment that, even for a brief moment, staved off the feelings of loneliness and rejection. I did admit that I had a small but strenuous hope that I would meet someone who would treat me as more than a passing enthusiasm, someone who wouldn't be overwhelmed by my past, a past that had exiled me from my own people. My own choices, such as they were, had confirmed me in my exile; but my thirst, I told him, was no different from anyone else's.

"Tell me what you thirst for," he said.

"Have you nowhere to go?" I asked.

He smiled. "Here is fine," he said. "I'm not looking to be anywhere else."

"Thanks," I muttered.

"Tell me," he said.

"About what I thirst for? Not much. At least I don't think it's very much. I want to love and be loved. I want to be taken seriously, not just taken to bed. I want to spend my life with a husband who'll pay attention to me and talk to me. I'm tired of spending a few breathless nights with tongue-tied runaways. Like everyone else I want the security of a home and family, not just a room filled with a dead woman's clutter. How would you like to live in a place of leftovers that no one comes back to, a dark room no one claims as home? It's lonely, very lonely."

"I know," he said. He put his hand on my shoulder for a moment. "I know," he repeated.

"Then you know what a mess my life is in. You know I'm devious and stupid and shallow, a hopeless case if ever there was one."

"Is that all you are?"

"Not much more," I said.

Above us a bird of prey wheeled, no doubt wondering if the still life below was ready for swiping. To stop myself from crying, I concentrated on the bird's round of inspection. Suddenly it came to a full stop, as if it had reached some secret destination in the stillness, lifted itself and hovered, ready to plunge. It looked so bold and free against the immensity of the empty sky, a thing of grandeur. But it was hunger, I reminded myself, that kept it where it was. All I was looking at was a huge hunger on the look-out. It dived, thought better of it, levelled itself, swung around in a wide sweep, and flew off to fix its practised stare on something else.

My throat was parched. I was dying for a drink. "Can you give me a drink?" I asked.

He looked up. "You're asking me for a drink?"

"I'm thirsty," I said. "Thirst brings us all to the well. Remember?" My voice trailed into nothing.

I waited for him to respond to my story or my request, but he just sat there in his own haze of wonder, fingering the end of his tunic. The heat and the silence didn't seem to bother him; all the same, I couldn't help wondering if I had said too much.

"The well," I croaked, "is the only thing in my life that gives me a reason for living. Take away the well and you cancel the only future that is left to me. It's all I have."

The old doubts came flooding back. Perhaps, like so many other men before him, he would excuse himself with that bogus charm that comes from a determination to be elsewhere. Or perhaps he would take refuge in his religion, after all, and reclaim the old reasons for rejecting the likes of me. For all our real differences, at least there was one thing we did share – our belief in the Messiah. I consoled myself in thinking we were together on that.

Still he said nothing. Perhaps he had nothing to say. I couldn't bear the silence and I made a last effort. "I know that the Messiah is coming," I said. "And when he comes he will explain everything. But he is still a long way off. Sometimes I wonder if the explanations will come too late. Too late to make any real difference."

I had run out of words. There was nothing more to be said. Why didn't he say anything?

He stood up. He's off, I thought, just as I feared. But he leaned over to the rope and started to lower the empty bucket into the well. When it reached the bottom, he tipped it expertly, then slowly pulled it out of the depths. When it came into view, the water was shimmering in the sunlight; it was running over, leaving large, round drops on the rope. He untied the handle and lifted the bucket to the ledge, then gestured for me to drink. I didn't need a second invitation. I rose quickly to my feet and crouched over the bucket. I drank hungrily and noisily and for long, like a wounded gazelle coming out of a parched land. Never had I known such thirstiness; never had I sensed such sheer relish in drinking water.

Only when I had finished drinking the water did he tell me who he was. At first I thought I must have been drunk from the water or dizzy from the oppressive heat; but I heard his revelation alright. He said it rather shyly, as if admitting some personal secret he might later regret having shared. At first, the enormity of his claim puzzled me, but then it delighted me. I was about to say something, but over his shoulder I could see some men approaching the well.

He turned around to see what had caught my attention.

"Whoever they are, they will be scandalised," I said.

He smiled and replied, "They are my crowd, and they will be."

He watched them as they joined us, almost daring them to say something. But whatever they were thinking, they kept it to themselves. They were disciples.

I knew it was time for me to go. I looked my thanks at him. He looked at his disciples and then looked at me. He walked over to me and kissed me on the cheek.

I turned and walked away from the well, and when I had gone a short distance I started to run as fast as I could towards the town. I was impelled by a new sense of urgency, trying to keep up with the thoughts racing through my head. I would tell the people I had met a man who introduced me to myself, I would tell them to run out to the well and bring him home before he disappeared forever. As I ran I imagined him coming to our town and speaking to all the people, imagined him drawing out the best in them, imagined him challenging them to forgive the likes of me.

Running up the shoulder of the hill to the town gates, my eyes filled with water, I could sense a living force welling up inside me.

A CHILD

My name is Mark bar Joachim. I have lots of friends and two sisters, all of whom are bigger than me. As everyone keeps telling me, I am small for my age – not only a child, but a miniature child. Tiddler is my nickname. I'm tired of people asking each other "Where's Tiddler?" when there I am, under their knees. I'm the only person I know who can get lost staying still. At the back of our house there is a line on the wall marking my height two years ago. It still does. I've thought of lowering it, just by about half a fingernail, but it wouldn't fool anyone – least of all my darling sisters.

My friends are a good bunch, but my sisters can be the biggest pains in Capernaum. They are twins. Double trouble. If ever there was a Miss Pain of Galilee contest, they would come joint first. Take this morning for instance. We all get together in the market-place, to play at something. Since we're all a bit tired of marriage games we decide on a good funeral. The problem is a willing corpse. I tell my sister Rachel to be dead and she tells me to get lost. She says she wants to play a hired musician, so she can play her flute and practise the dirges she's been learning. She plays rotten. Then, sure as fate, my sister Elizabeth says that she too wants to play her flute and that I should play dead. She has her arms crossed, the way Mum does when she says something important. Just to make sure I get the point, Beth says that if I don't play dead she will kill me.

See what I mean about my sisters?

Anyway, I give in, just like Dad does when Mum gets on her high horse. We decide to use my fishing net and two long sticks to make the funeral litter for me to lie dead on. Benjamin's dad is a carpenter, so Benji runs home to get the sticks. Beth tells me to go home and get the two flutes and my net. "And get something for a shroud," she shouts after me. She's great at giving orders. Why God made her with such a huge mouth is one of life's unsolved mysteries.

When I reach home Mum is just beginning to bake some cakes on the fire outside the house. I ask her if it's all right to borrow Dad's old cloak to use as a shroud for our game. She laughs and says it's so moth-eaten and patched that even the dead wouldn't wear it. "But be sure, Mark, to bring it back," she says. "Otherwise you won't have a blanket for the cold nights." For all her generosity, Mum throws away nothing, believing that everything will prove useful some day. After trying unsuccessfully to borrow a couple of the cakes, I collect the net and the cloak and the flutes to take back with me.

I'm really proud of my net, it's my favourite thing in the whole world. It was part of an old fishing net, too torn to be mended, that Dad brought home from work. He left some of the sinkers on, weights that I had helped him tie on. I spent an age mending the thing. Every time I lift the net to my nose and close my eyes I can smell the sea and the fish and the boats. It has the same smell as Dad's clothes, a grown-up smell, kind of important. I hope I smell like that when I grow up.

When I approach the market-place the others start

shouting, "Hurry up, Tiddler!" Rachel and Beth ask if I have the flutes, so I hand over the instruments of torture wrapped in Dad's old cloak. We lay out the net on the ground, double it over, then carefully work Benji's two sticks through the mesh. The litter is ready.

The girls in the group want to wash me and anoint me with their perfume, but I tell them I'm not one of their dolls. Besides, I'm not dead yet. John says that he could be a Roman soldier and kill me with his sword. John used to be my best friend. Since I'm the one that is dying I insist on choosing my own death. After serious thought I announce that I'm going to die from eating too many cakes with mint in them. Then I pretend to choke, wobble, clutch at Benji's shirt and finally fall stone dead. It hurts like mad when I fall.

The racket I make is so good that a couple of old women leave off trying to sell their figs and come over to ask what's wrong. Out of the corner of my eye I can see them peering down at me. When the others explain that I am only pretend dead, the women look embarrassed. One of them scratches her behind and says to the other: "Kids! Who'd have them?" Point made, they waddle back to their figs.

We get back to the serious business of funerals. My hands and feet are tied with two of the girls' ribbons. The girls wrap the shroud around me, and Miriam, whom I rather like, tries to tickle me. I stay cool. Four of my pals lift me onto the litter, and when they lift me off the ground everyone starts to wail and cry for poor me. We're off.

The two fig women give us looks that would wither a cactus.

The girls head our procession. At our funerals, women walk in front of the litter – something to do with Eve bringing death into the world, so women must lead its victims to the grave. Strange, but there you are. When Rachel and Beth start playing a dirge in perfect disharmony, I begin to wonder if poor Eve is also blamed for inventing the flute.

The market-place is unusually quiet, so we have no difficulty making our way past the sellers and avoiding their wares, spread out on ground cloaks. The wails of our funeral procession compete with the cries of the market sellers, who give us disapproving looks for mocking such a serious business as death. Some grown-ups seem to spend so much energy frowning upon life, you wonder why they get up in the morning.

The market inspector, the one who told Mum she was overcharging for her mint cakes, orders us to go away and play somewhere else. The procession speeds up. We don't get very far because I fall through the net and hurt my bum. We all laugh. Rachel says to me: "Keep quiet and close your eyes, silly, you're supposed to be dead." Rachel can't even leave the dead in peace. I keep quiet while they fix everything. It takes ages. I'm worried about my net.

When we get started up again, I pray to God not to send me to heaven until I'm much older than Dad. Heaven must be hugely boring with all those dead people lying on clouds, their hands and feet tied up, their eyes closed, but their ears left open so they can listen to the flutes. Under my breath I warn God that he'd better not give flutes to Rachel and Beth when they get there, otherwise he'll have an almighty walk-out on his hands.

Everyone is making a nice big racket as we go down the road to the lake. I don't want to open my eyes in case I am thumped, but I sort of notice a big crowd gathered at the landing where the fishing boats come in. I can hear a man's voice addressing the crowd, and when we get nearer some people start telling us to shut up and go away.

We are disturbing their grown-up meeting.

My friends stop wailing, my sisters stop playing their flutes. I look up. All my mourners look a mess because they have been picking up dust from the road and putting it on their hair – the way grown-ups do during a funeral procession. Except that my mourners have put on fistfuls of the stuff, to express their deep loss at my sudden departure. We must look a real sight.

I can now see the man who is addressing the crowd. He is standing on the prow of one of the fishing boats, free from the press of the crowd. It is Jesus, the holy man who lives at big Simon's house.

Suddenly two men emerge from the crowd and come over to us. They look serious. One of them says: "What do you kids think you're doing here? This is no place for you. Beat it. And do it quietly."

Jesus stops addressing the crowd and calls to the two bouncers: "Boanerges!" They turn to face him. "Bring the children here. Don't send them away." He tells the crowd to make way for us and let us through to the front.

By this time Rachel and Beth are crying their eyes out. They're scared. Me too, because I think we're in for a public telling-off. I feel daft, still being carried in the litter, and start praying that Dad isn't in the crowd. We go through the crowd, past all the staring faces, right up to the front. Everyone looks at us like we've messed up their whole morning. I promise God I'll never play at funerals again if he gets me out of this. Jesus is smiling at us, like he is having a good time.

My bearers put me down on the landing-stage. I'm not sure if I should get up, so I decide to stay down. Maybe nobody will notice me. Jesus climbs out of the boat and comes across to us. I think maybe he is just smiling before he raps us. He kneels down beside me.

Wait for it, I think, here comes trouble.

"How is my dead friend?" Jesus asks me.

"I'm all right, really. Thanks. I'm sorry to mess up your meeting."

"Don't worry, you haven't messed up anything. What's your name?"

"Mark bar Joachim, but some people call me Tiddler. Because I'm so small."

"My name is Jesus. I get called all sorts of names, too. Listen, Mark, I need your help with something important."

"Me?"

"Yes, you. But first, let's get you up from there."

Jesus lifts the shroud off me and hands it to Benji. He unties the ribbons from my hands and feet. He lifts me out of the litter and carries me on his shoulders, right onto the boat. He sits me on top of the prow, facing out to the crowd. I look out at a sea of upturned faces, all staring at me. They all look puzzled, wondering what is going on. Everything is so quiet. All you can hear is the lapping of the water against the landing-stage. Then Jesus, his hands on my shoulders, starts talking to the crowd.

"We welcome the little visitors into our midst. As our ears can testify, they wail extremely well. But as our eyes can see, they are afraid of us now. They fear our rejection and hostility. They haven't come to interrupt my teaching about the kingdom of God; rather, their arrival throws light on a truth at the heart of the kingdom.

"Look at this child here. His name is Mark. Take a good look at him. Unless you can welcome this little child you cannot welcome the kingdom of God.

"I tell you solemnly: never despise littleness, because in littleness God hides the greatness of his kingdom.

"Never scorn the poor because they have no money, nor the simple because they have no influence. To such as these the kingdom of God is given.

"Never despise the wretched because their spirits are crushed, nor the maimed because their bodies are broken. To such as these the kingdom of God is given.

"Never spurn the weak because they are caught in sin, nor the sick because they have been laid low by affliction. To such as these the kingdom of God is given.

"Never shrink from the lonely because they live in the absence of love, nor the stranger who is kept from the embrace of welcome. To such as these the kingdom of God is given.

"Always treat others, no matter who they are, as you would like them to treat you. That is the meaning of the Law and the Prophets.

"Love each other kindly, love each other respectfully, love each other generously.

"Remember this child, remember him well. Welcome him and you make room in your hearts for the kingdom of God."

By the time Jesus is finished speaking I have a smile on my face as broad as the river Jordan. I just can't help it. Imagine! People have to welcome the Tiddlers of this world. I hope Rachel and Beth have been paying attention, though I suppose Jesus was meaning them to be included among the little ones. We are important to Jesus. And, after all, he is really good and holy and all that.

Jesus hands me down to big Simon, who tells me I am a big fish now. No kidding! He says that in front of everyone. Then he tells our group to carry on with the game we were playing, so I get back into my place, to be dead again. But this time I keep my eyes open. Rachel and Beth smile at me and start playing their flutes. They don't sound too bad this time – must be a miracle which Jesus worked on the quiet.

As we set off again I wave to Jesus and he waves back. All the grown-ups make way for us, and I can see Dad smiling. When I pass him he hooks my nose with two fingers and shakes it – the way he does when he's pleased. I sit up and smile at everyone as I'm carried out beyond the last line of people.

When we get up the road a bit we have to stop our game because we're all laughing too much to play at funerals. Benji is laughing so much that the dust is falling out of his hair. They all ask me what it was like, and I tell them how smashing it was looking out over all those grown-ups and how I could even see the bald patch on big Simon's head.

Miriam doesn't say anything. She just keeps looking at me like I'm some kind of wonderboy or something. When we finish laughing I pick up my net and Dad's old cloak. On the way home with Rachel and Beth I tell them that when Jesus gets to God's age then heaven will be a lot less boring. The twins agree.

A WOMAN
OF MAGDALA

I don't know if you've ever been to my home town of Magdala – it's on the west shore of the lake of Galilee. Beautiful it is, without a doubt, backed by green fertile land, facing the blue and lovely lake. Magdala means "the fish-tower" – well named since many of the locals work either fishing the lake or salting the fish and taking them to markets as far away as Joppa. Before Herod Antipas built Tiberias, Magdala was the principal town on the west shore: having our own hippodrome marked us out as something more than just highland fisherfolk. We are main road people. We are no strangers to Greek life and leisure. We are cosmopolitan, forward-looking, disposed to change. We are lakeside Galileans.

All the lakeside towns are busy, not just with local folks but with travellers and tax-collectors and Roman soldiers and entertainers and smugglers and runaways. All sorts. In Galilee we're bordered on three sides by foreigners, making the region a real cross-roads. Galilee of the Gentiles. The traffic of the world passes through here, you know, which produces a hospitality industry. All this traffic needs servicing, of course, and that has turned Magdala into a playground for fugitives. When it comes to handling human traffic, Magdala has the knack.

Some of the traffic stops at my door. I am well known

in the district as a lady of the night, a hospitality mistress, a whore, a sure address for Roman soldiers on rest and recreation. I used to work in one of the roadside inns that specialise in having a staff of "little she-asses" for the comfort of customers, but it wasn't long before I was able to set up my own place. I have a faithful band of followers who are overwhelmed by my sensitive skills. Nobody, however, wants to be my neighbour. Most of the locals despise me as a collector of human debris, a man-eater with a catholic appetite. Sometimes the grizzled women of the town, haggard with the disappointment life has dealt them, will shout insults at me in the street. Perhaps their contempt is a form of envy or a means of defence. Perhaps they suppose that I enjoy delight after different delight while they are pledged to endure the same awkward aching transaction night after eternal night. Who knows? I only know that I am in no position to judge them.

My clients have ranged from the courteous to the weird: the young legionary, childish and endearing, who comes to listen to the tales of an experienced woman in the hope that one day this useless knowledge will lead him to command performances; the fish-merchant, loud with the stink of dead catches, who likes being netted and landed with dispatch; the shy hopeless priest, worshipped by a pious wife, who shells out good money for me to defile his sacred territory; the shepherds on a market day, investing in a new memory to break the monotony of their dreary luckless lives. There are the lusty ones and the lewd ones, the bad ones and the sad ones, a procession of hopefuls who arrive at my door looking for some temporary relief.

I have never looked for their love or offered them mine: we know the limitations of our own resources.

In my profession I have learned never to disclose what

I know about people, what I really feel, what hurts me, or what haunts me. I am inscrutable to my customers, the soul of grand detachment. I suspect that none of them is disposed to bother anyway, since the questions I am asked (Why do you do it? Have you ever thought of getting married?) are just to decorate the anxious time before and after business. So, I moan and shudder and smile and groan to order. A nightly ritual of mime. I am flawless when it comes to sending my customers away happy. I am all things to all men, and I send them away with the satisfaction of the truly zonked. I know, however, that if they are ever discovered by their wives, the first thing they will wail will be: "But it didn't mean anything." How right they will be.

Being a whore does nothing for your sense of dignity. You might say that if I was all that worried about my dignity I'd never have become a whore. But no matter who you are, my friend, you ache to believe in your own dignity and worth. Whether you are a high priest or a whore, a Pharisee or a tax collector, you hold on to this restless claim that you have some secret self that is more than all the silly disguises you adopt to fool the watching world. Only one man has helped to give substance to this secret yearning in me. He is a fellow Galilean, Jesus of Nazareth.

When he came to visit me here in the late afternoon, I was working in the garden, tending the sweet-scented jasmine. From behind me I heard a voice say how lovely the garden looked; when I turned to see who was speaking, the stranger added, as if by way of admission, that he wasn't much of a gardener himself. Small talk, I thought. The carob tree, with its hanging clusters of red berries and long pods, caught his eye. He walked over to it and felt the texture of the pods: he looked hungry enough to eat them.

At first I thought he must be a desperate client, so I

suggested he came back at dusk when my surgery hours started. Then he told me who he was and why he had come. I was intrigued by his simplicity and candour, to say nothing of his nerve, though I was wary of his motives. So this was Jesus of Nazareth, nervously fingering the roses around the door, hardly up to his reputation as an upstart Galilean with a talent for confrontation. I warned him that his standing as a prophet would take a dive when word got around that he had sought me out, but he just smiled and asked me if I was going to keep him on the doorstep forever.

What could I do? I invited the man who invited himself, into my house.

Inside it was dark and cool. He sat on the low couch beneath the window, the very place where I have laid down so many fruitless memories. I offered him a drink, pomegranate juice or wine, and he opted for the wine. His eyes started taking in the room as if searching for a clue to the character of the owner. I brought out my best metal wine-cup, put a freshly baked round of bread on a plate, filled a jug from the pitcher of wine and another jug with water.

When I placed all this before him, he said, "Another cup would not go amiss."

"Prophets don't eat with the likes of me," I said.

"Bring another cup," he said. "I've never liked eating alone."

When I brought it, he said the blessing and I heard again words that had been lost to me since childhood. As I watched him mix the deep purple wine with water, as I had watched so many of my guests do before him, I wondered if he would be able to hold on to his reason for visiting. He broke the bread, held out a piece for me, and then handed me a cup of wine.

We ate and drank together, him and me.

He started to talk about himself, how he grew up in the small town of Nazareth, which he had learned to love; but no matter how much he loved the place and its people, he said, home life could not content him or contain him. He felt impelled to leave home and go south to see the prophet John the Baptist, who helped him take a new direction in life. When he spoke of John, it was with the reverence people normally reserve for the great rabbis. After his time with John, he went home; but his return only brought pain and disappointment. His own people of Nazareth could not bring themselves to accept the change they saw in him.

"So," he said, "I had to leave again, for different reasons. Going back home confirmed me in my original decision to leave it. It's funny how the choices we make in life can take us, gradually but surely, away from the very place we thought belonged to us forever."

"But you wouldn't have stayed, anyway," I said.

"No," he said, "but it's good to know you belong some place and can return there. I can't go back to Nazareth."

"You shouldn't be surprised at the people's reaction," I said. "It's much easier having a carpenter around the house than a prophet, easier to talk of broken chairs than broken lives. Believe me, I know what I'm saying."

He laughed and took another drink of wine. Warming to his subject, he went on to tell me that his message was simple: God loves the world and wants everyone to be at peace with him and each other. Love and forgiveness, he insisted, are the only real forces for change; they are the only things that can free people from the grip of their sinful past. As he spoke he shared his understanding of what so many of us are at pains to conceal: that we are all anxious, vulnerable, unsure, lonely, tired, sinful, ridiculous. But not unimportant. He spoke of God as a Father whose arms are strong enough to hug people into importance, whose heart is big enough to welcome everyone, and whose love will always scandalise people with the strangeness of its choices.

"But look at me," I said to him. "I've settled for a life that puts me beyond the reach or interest of God, to say nothing of God's kind of people. If I gave up my clients and went to the synagogue on the sabbath, they'd hang me by my hair from the women's gallery. Who would blame them? I've got a bad name all over the town, and nothing will shift that. No matter what I do, I'll always be the whore of Magdala."

"But," he got as far as saying.

"No buts, Jesus," I interrupted him. "If your crowd in Nazareth wanted to relieve you of the burden of living, think what the crowd in Magdala would do to me! And you're not exactly anyone's idea of a public sinner, are you? Though that might change when word gets around you've been here. Visiting me is dangerous to your health."

"I know that and I must live with it, but it's your health I'm concerned about. That's why I'm here."

"I appreciate that, but you don't seem to appreciate that I am a serious sinner, fully paid up. I'm not boasting, believe me, but I'm not your average sinner who fails periodically and then struggles to do better. I am accomplished at sin, familiar with it, committed to it. I don't know anything else but sin. Sin is me. You're looking at it."

"Do you believe in God's forgiveness?" he asked.

"Not when it comes to selling sex, no."

"Do you believe God loves you?"

"Me?" I laughed. "God's no fool. He doesn't waste his love on lost causes. Love is not to waste, is it?"

"Why do you restrict God? Why do you have to set limits on his love? Love never reckons with how it is wasted, it moves out of its own freedom to give. How love is received is not love's problem, is it? God's love doesn't control us, it doesn't demand its own completion, it risks rejection. When God offers you love, all he can do is wait. You are in control of God's love: that is God's vulnerability."

"How can you talk of the almighty being vulnerable?"

"Because he is love. Almighty love is almighty vulnerable. God cannot but love, and his love is endless. That's why he forgives endlessly."

"I'd love to believe that as I'd love to change my life, but I honestly don't have the resources for either. There's so much for God to forgive and so little chance of me loving him in return."

"Can I tell you a story?" he asked.

"A story? If you want. I hear them all the time."

He looked hurt. "Not that kind of story."

"Sorry, go ahead."

"Once there was a certain money lender who had two men in his debt. One owed him five hundred denarii, the other fifty. Neither of them could pay him, so he pardoned them both."

"Lucky men," I said.

"Tell me this: which of them will love the money lender more?"

"The one who was pardoned more, obviously."

"Exactly."

"But that's only..."

"No buts," he interrupted me. He reached out to me, taking my hands and pressing them firmly. "Mary, Mary," he said, "if you have ears, listen to what I'm saying to you."

"I am listening and I do appreciate your kindness and sympathy. Believe me, I do. It's just that I don't think you've grasped how frightful my life really is."

"Why do people think that because I'm sympathetic I must be obtuse?"

He stopped talking. For a long time I said nothing. I didn't know what to say. My mouth felt dried up; it was an effort just to swallow. I didn't know what I was supposed to do. Never in my life had I felt so entirely the centre of a man's attention, which may sound strange coming from me. As if sensing my awkwardness, he released his hold on my hands, rose from the couch, and crossed the room to the open door. He stood there, looking out over the lake.

Dusk was beginning to fall. From where I sat it looked as if some vast undefined grief was descending upon the treetops and seeping into the lake. Far off in the fields somewhere there was the sound of children's voices and their easy laughter, the distant report of other lives. I rose from the stool and filled the two lamps. After lighting them, the sweetish smell of olive oil started to spread throughout the room.

I sat down again. I sensed that if I did not speak now, I would regret it for many a day. I heard him turning from the door and returning to his seat on the couch. Still he said not a word. He was going to wait out the silence.

I heard myself speak – in a funny way at first, as if I were a mere witness to my own predicament. Gradually, I gained confidence and for the first time in my life I talked about myself and what I had come to.

From the beginning, I told him, I was marked for moral ambiguity, if not for collapse. That had nothing to do with my family or my upbringing or my surroundings. Since I was thirteen, I said, I've known I possessed a strange something, a drawing power that attracted men's attention. It was difficult to define this exactly, but I knew it was there. I knew I wasn't beautiful in the same way that other girls could be. Their emphatic beauty made them distant, somehow, like perfectly formed sculptures, flawless works of art. They were admired instantly and forgotten instantly, leaving no ache of remembrance to stir up men's nervous longings. These beautiful ones always seemed to aim for marriage, I said, and that institution of bondage contained them for life. My beauty, spare as it was, seemed to appeal directly to whatever raw and immediate desires lodge in men's stomachs. I didn't know then what these desires were. Who knows, anyway, what strange compulsions we appeal to in other people? All I knew was that I had an energy in me that turned men's heads and made their eyes narrow in yearning, yearning, yearning.

I wasn't aware of doing anything to arouse men's sexual interest; it was something there in me, a dangerous talent. It was as if there was another physical creature inside me who threatened to take control, a creature who knew with terrible authority that men were at her mercy.

So, I explained, early in my life it was already too late.

I did not know if this was making any sense to Jesus. I remember saying, almost pleading: "I'm not trying to justify anything; I'm just trying to find a language for the mess I'm in now. My life has been a drift to here. Trying to make that drift into a story is trying to impose order on a scatter of events that didn't have any. That's the way it's been for me, perhaps that's the way it is for many. Days go by, people come and go, months pass, time moves on, all without much contrivance, and we wake up one day to find ourselves stuck in the middle of life. Too late we realise we have missed the boat. After a while a sense of inevitability seems to infect everything. I doubt if we have come to where we are in our lives as a result of much free choice. We become what is left for us, the remains of things."

I then took Jesus on a guided tour of the ruins of my life. I missed nothing. I disguised nothing. And as he sat and listened to my story, without comment or interruption, he gave me the impression that every word I spoke was a gift and that he knew the pain and the release in the telling.

When I had finished, he leaned over to me and again took my hands in his, holding them as if to press home what he was going to say. He began to pray. He did not rehearse my many sins, he did not dote on my history of stupidities, but cast all that aside to appeal to the goodness in me. He let me know that wrongdoing was not the whole story about me, that time was not a necessary continuation of all that had been, rather an opportunity for what could be.

"Now is the opportune time," he said. "Now."

The experience of being forgiven is difficult to describe. The way some people forgive leaves you feeling worse off than before, because they so insist on your wrongdoing that their forgiveness looks like domination. The way some people forgive is sinful. With Jesus it was different. I felt forgiven not because he spoke words of forgiveness but because I believed his kind of love made forgiveness inevitable. It was his love that made the difference. My sins could not outstrip his love. I mattered to him more than my many sins, therefore I was forgiven. That is why, for me, his words counted. He was in what he said.

But even as I began to feel unburdened of my past, I felt afraid of the future. Would it last? Would it be business as usual after he had gone? Sitting beside him,

I prayed that this experience would not be a fleeting enchantment and that tomorrow it would be there.

He was speaking to me again, saying that he wanted me to think of an offer. He asked me if I would be interested in joining his travelling mission. I was taken aback. Me? With the likes of me in his group, he'd become the laughing-stock of the whole region. I said that I wasn't that zealous about the prospect of washing men's shirts or cooking for crowds, but he laughed and told me not to worry – I would find my place and discover what I could give. Deep down I was flattered out of my sandals! I am dying to get away from here. I am poised for flight. I felt excited at the prospect of a future far away from all this madness and misery. Imagine: I was being asked to join a group of people who would care what would become of me, just as I would surely learn to care for them.

Jesus did not ask for my answer immediately. "Tomorrow evening," he said, "I'll be dining at the house of Simon the Pharisee. You can let me know then what you think."

I promised him that I would give him my answer at Simon's house.

As he rose to leave, I offered to show him out the back door – I knew that my customers would be hanging around the front and they would be certain to misinterpret his visit. He moved to the front door. Without another word he walked out and headed off in the direction of the lake. He had only the infinitesimal light of the stars to go by.

I closed the door and pushed home the bolt. Tomorrow, I thought. Would I be able to defect, leave behind my allegiance to habit, cross over to him? Or would I return to giving what I knew I could, snatches of love at bargain prices? I felt exhausted, spent, emptied out. It was as if there was nothing left inside me but a large vacancy. I knew I could not sleep.

It is beginning to grow light now. Another day, his tomorrow, is here. When I open the front door I let in the east wind, cold and dry, blowing off the lake. The force of it snuffs out the lights. From where I stand in the doorway I can just make out the shape of four fishing boats returning from their night's catch. I see them, lose them, then see them again as they appear through clear patches in the dawn mist. They look strangely insubstantial in this setting, like ghost ships drifting out of their element, ill at ease in the gathering light.

I pull my shawl tighter around my shoulders.

For a while I continue to watch the slow progress of the boats making for harbour. Gradually they seem to become more real, their shape becoming more defined. I hear a faint sound coming over the lake, carried on the wind. It's the sound of chanting. I listen. The fishermen are singing the song of the catch, a prelude to the sure sale they will make on landing. They have worked hard all night and caught plenty. Good luck to them.

All of a sudden a feeling of great emptiness comes over me and a remembered pain comes back to make itself felt anew. Once, when I was a child, my friends played a cruel trick on me: during a game of hide-and-seek they told me it was my turn to go and hide, but instead of seeking me out they all ran off to the next village to play a different game. I remember how long it took me to admit to myself that I remained undiscovered not because I was clever at hiding but because no one was looking for me. Some game.

I have this acute sense of being stranded, left behind by other lives intent on fulfilment elsewhere, abandoned by those who find refuge in the interminable round of hope, half-hope, disappointment.

I feel myself begin to shiver. I come back inside, into the warmth, and close the door behind me. The dark is total. I must try to get some sleep now. Today is the day. I lie down on the couch and settle myself as comfortably as I can. I close my eyes. I can no longer hear the fishermen's chant, only the sound of my own breathing. If only I can rest before I go to Simon's house, before I go to the place of the answer. I pull the shawl up over my ears.

SIMON THE PHARISEE

I am a man of few words, not given to writing or to easy conversation, so I shall endeavour to be brief. Allow me first, if I may, to introduce myself: I am a Hebrew born of Hebrews, a Pharisee by vocation, a civil servant by profession, a husband of a dutiful wife, a father of two young sons. Even though God in his infinite wisdom has called me to belong to the religious party of the separated ones – regarded in some quarters as "stuffy and exclusive" – I think of myself and my Pharisaism as open to new religious insight. Indeed, that is why, five days ago, I ventured to invite Jesus of Nazareth to my house for a meal. He kindly acceded to my request and promised to come after he had preached at the synagogue service on the sabbath.

I am not, as I have already intimated, a man who can put people at ease in conversation, so I invited seven other guests, all Pharisees, whose intelligence and ability to converse would ensure that the meal would not be a social disappointment. They all agreed, two of them reluctantly since they had serious reservations about the possible outcome.

"I'm not sure I entirely approve of the idea," Kareah said. "Jesus may be a good man, but his unpredictability makes him a religious risk. Anything could happen."

"I agree," Chenaanah added. "If it emerges later that Jesus opposes everything we hold dear, we'll end up looking very foolish. I'll come, Simon, but we have to be cautious. We have to live in Magdala after he's gone."

I confess I was surprised at their hesitancy; but as my wife said to me yesterday when I declined to share her nervousness about the whole enterprise: "Simon, you're too dull to get nervous about anything!" My wife is given to such jovial asides.

She seemed more relaxed, however, by the time my eight guests had taken their place at table. She had arranged three low tables in banquet form: the upper table faced out to the open courtyard, and the other two tables adjoined it, one on either side. Each table was set, on one side only, for three people. My place was in the middle of the upper table with Jesus on my right and Kareah on my left.

In front of each place my wife had placed individual couches, to facilitate our custom at formal meals of eating in a recumbent posture, leaning on one's left elbow, leaving the right hand free for food and drink. When the blessing had been pronounced and the wine poured, my wife bowed and retired to oversee the servants.

I picked a choice piece of lamb, dipped it into a dish of mint sauce, and handed it to Jesus. The meal had begun.

The dinner started off well. Everyone was amiable, charming, polite; each guest seemed anxious to create an atmosphere of respectful ease appropriate to the occasion. Jesus behaved so creditably that even Kareah appeared minimally relaxed, alert as he was to anything approaching theological surprise. The unexpected made him feel incompetent.

From my place at table I could see a small group gathered in the courtyard, to watch the proceedings and listen into the conversation, and I admit I was pleased that our dinner had attracted such interest.

As the conversation flowed I was working up to the point of making a witticism – on some topic that now entirely eludes me – when a woman entered the dining room, looked at each of us in turn, and without a word of explanation proceeded to walk behind the guests until she came to a stop behind Jesus. Something happened in Kareah's throat that sounded akin to choking. Everyone knew the woman as a local prostitute. I was appalled. Just as I was about to charge the servants to remove this blight from our midst, Jesus turned around and smiled at her. Smiled at her, I tell you!

When this happened, the woman started to weep, and as her sobbing became more guttural her whole body began to shiver and shake in a manner consistent with epileptic demoniacism. She dropped to her knees, fell forward and wept all over Jesus' feet, clutching his ankles as if the contact would somehow pacify her trembling body.

I was unsure how to react to these hysterical convulsions – taking place, if you please, on my dining room floor – since any display of disapproval or unwarranted fuss would have embarrassed my guest of honour. He looked utterly unperturbed, however, as if frantic theatrics of this kind happened regularly at picnics and dinner parties he attended. Not for him the discomfiture of the righteous, the indignation of propriety. Jesus looked a willing partner in this strange duet, so much so that I thought he and the woman might be engaging in some arcane form of affectionate sport unknown to the rest of us. Whatever was going on, I did believe, as I am sure you will, that a dinner table is not the place for such distressingly physical entanglements.

My guests, all men of exemplary character and faultless

decorum, were naturally rendered speechless by this vulgar display, but they struggled to betray no emotion whatsoever. They had, of course, stopped eating as soon as the dreadful creature appeared, for her presence, believe me, was no stimulant to appetite. Indeed, the presence of a woman like this in the same room would normally have propelled my guests to the nearest exit, and thence to a cleansing bath. Had they excused themselves and left the house, I would not have been surprised. Caught as they were by their own unfailing kindness and politeness, their good manners masked their disapproval: a row of raised eyebrows and reproachful looks were soon converted into custody of the eyes.

As I dared glance behind me I could see the woman was using her long hair to wipe away her tears from the feet of Jesus. Not satisfied with that, she then proceeded to kiss his feet and pour some unguent on them from a small perfume flask she was carrying around her neck. There was an intense and sickly smell from the ointment, which seemed to spill out and fill the whole room.

What I could not comprehend was this: how could Jesus indulge such a libertine? Did he have no history of dealing with shameless women who threw themselves at him, demanding affection for their tearful, artless advances? Was he so deprived of emotional support that he needed to welcome such crude advances in public? More importantly, if Jesus were a real prophet he would surely have known what sort of a woman was touching him, for she was known throughout the region as an accomplished sinner. How could a prophet allow himself to be caressed and defiled by such a woman? Could he not see her touch was deadly?

As if he read my thoughts, Jesus turned and said to me:

"Simon, I have something to say to you." His tone sounded critical, lacking its earlier cordiality.

"Speak, Teacher," I said.

"Once upon a time there was a money lender who had two men in his debt; one owed him five hundred denarii, the other fifty. When they could not pay, he freely forgave them both. Which of them will love him more?"

I struggled for a moment or two to accommodate this oblique intervention. Why, I wondered, was my attention being transposed to never-never-land?

"The one who was pardoned more, I suppose," I replied.

"You have judged rightly," Jesus said.

With respect, what did that have to do with anything? Why were we suddenly discussing moral fiction when a real disaster was happening under our noses and ruining our dinner party? I did not say this, of course, unwilling as I was to exacerbate an already shameful situation. Besides, I had the beginning of a pain in my head.

"The unworthy food I have set before you needs attention," I said. "Let us eat."

I hoped that the woman would leave off her unwanted ministrations and go back to wherever she came from; I hoped my guests would turn their attention to eating. When I looked at my fellow Pharisees, I met their unresponsive gaze. The seven of them looked like they had just received notice of a grave illness. None of them appeared willing to make the effort: their discomfort had displaced whatever appetite they had, and they no doubt believed that the meal was beyond redemption anyway. I could not attach blame to them; it was the woman who had stolen the ease we had hitherto shared together, and she was making no move to go. An air of dereliction had settled over the room.

At this point Jesus turned around and faced the woman.

I thought he was going to say something to her, for neither of them had spoken a word to each other. But instead, he addressed me as he continued to look at her.

"Simon, do you see this woman?"

Did I see this woman? I ask you! How could anyone miss seeing a prostitute-cum-foot-fetishist perform at his own dinner table? How could anyone not see this primitive creature from miles away? I looked to my other guests for help.

"Simon," Jesus said.

"Yes?"

"Do you see this woman?"

"Master," I heard myself pleading.

"Look at her, Simon. When I came into your house, you gave me no water for my feet, but she has wet my feet with her tears and wiped them away with her hair. You gave me no kiss, but she has been covering my feet with kisses ever since I came in. You did not anoint my head with oil, but she has anointed my feet with ointment. Can't you see, Simon?"

When you have just been compared to your discredit with a prostitute, in your own house, in front of your friends and family and servants, it is mighty difficult to see anything but red.

"See what, Teacher?" I managed to ask.

"Can't you see that this woman's many sins must have been forgiven her, or she would not be showing such great love? The man who is forgiven little, shows little love."

I said nothing.

Then, still looking at the woman, Jesus addressed her directly: "Your sins have been forgiven."

At this, my other guests could not contain themselves any longer, and they started to murmur among themselves:

"Who does he think he is? Who is this man who also forgives sins?"

For his part, Jesus kept looking at the woman. He smiled at her and said, "Your faith has saved you, go in peace."

Before going, she leaned over to Jesus, in the fashion of one who has lost all reserve, and whispered something in his left ear. As I brushed away her long wet hair from where it fell, momentarily, on my shoulder, I could only make out the word "answer". Whatever she said to Jesus, it visibly pleased him, for he nodded his head and smiled at her. I watched him continue to smile at her as she rose, adjusted herself, and began retracing her steps; I watched him look after her as she made her way past the guests, carrying herself as if she were a woman whose price was above rubies; I watched him follow her with his eyes as she eased her way through the onlookers in the courtyard, turned for the main door, and disappeared as abruptly as she had come.

Only when she had gone did Jesus seem to remember he was a guest at dinner table and compose himself accordingly. His unsmiling gaze now travelled around all the faces fixed upon him. When he had taken us all in, he smiled to himself and reached for his cup of wine. He first raised it to eye level as if he wanted to inspect the fragile quality of my Roman glass, then drank what wine there was in the cup. As I watched him, a curious thought struck me: I could not be certain, of course, but I suspected that what he was really doing was offering a silent toast to the woman who had just showered him with such lavish devotion.

For myself, I prayed to God that we had seen the last of her.

To say that the rest of the dinner passed off tolerably well would be to strain the limits of language. It was a quiet disaster. We never really recovered from the frightful interruption, and we filled the remaining time, which was blessedly brief, between exchanging polite nothings and practising the art of inscrutability. It was clear to a blind man that no one at table wanted to linger for a moment longer than civility or good manners required. Even Jesus was quiet.

Things were so dull that, by the end of the meal, there was only one outsider left in the courtyard. No doubt the others had gone off to tell the story in the neighbourhood, eager to broadcast the scandalous mix-up that happened when the Pharisee and the prophet and the prostitute collided at dinner. The remaining solitary witness sat rather forlornly behind a pillar. Perhaps he had no one to tell.

When the guests took their leave, making agonizingly polite remarks as they escaped to their various sanctuaries, I felt nothing but relief to see the end of the whole sorry enterprise. Closing the outer doors after the last guest, I told my wife it would be some time before we risked another ambitious dinner party with a mystery guest. Ambition and mystery, she told me, should be confined to the menu; she had no heart for anarchy at dinner table. She looked exhausted.

As I stood in the courtyard and watched her ascend the stairs, she called back to me: "Simon, come to bed. There is nothing you can do now."

"I doubt I will sleep," I replied. "I shall be up presently."

"Then I shall say goodnight," she said, turning the corner of the stairs.

"Goodnight," I said. "And thank you for all your good work."

But she was already gone.

The house is quiet now. Everyone has retired. Rather than opting for bed and oblivion, I am drawn back to the scene of the crime and re-enter the empty dining room. I sit down at my place at table, with a jug of wine for company, and stare at the vacated couches around me like I am waiting for a gathering of ghosts. As I review the unlikely connivance between Jesus and the woman, the awkwardness of my friends, my own hesitancy before inquisition, I feel like someone who has wandered into the wrong story. Did all this happen here? My nose tells me it surely did. The aroma of the woman's perfume lingers in the air like a defiant memento of her trespass.

I pour myself another glass of wine. How many of the guests appreciated this choice wine which I reserve for special occasions? So much for the lost details of hospitality, I think. I sip the wine, grateful in a world of uncertainties for the assurance of its warmth.

I blame myself, of course, for foolishly assuming I could bring Jesus and Pharisaism together, for thinking tolerance to be easy, for exposing dear friends to my misplaced hopes. The only certain thing I seem to have achieved is to have brought shame on my house. Could I have acted differently?

I realise, not being entirely dim witted, that Jesus was challenging me to see more to the woman than her many sins, to see her attentions not as the defiling caresses of a whore but as the tender and insistent expression of a repentant woman. But I am a child of my own religious formation: I possess an inherited caution when it comes to matters such as change, believing we need more proof of conversion than a prolonged emotional outburst. Her tears were many, certainly, but they did not make a pool deep enough for the cleansing immersion of such a life.

Believe me when I say that I do not wish the woman

any harm; indeed, on the contrary, I would be happy if she turned away form her perversity and devoted herself to good works. I say this because I believe there is no limit to the resourcefulness of God, but the favour of the Almighty must be maintained by our righteous choices and repaid with interest. Whatever choices the woman may make, whatever new roads she may travel on, have nothing to do with me, and I fail to see how my life is connected to hers. I am not responsible for her.

The way I behaved towards the woman was governed by the wise sayings of Solomon son of David:

> My son, be attentive to my wisdom,
> incline your ear to my understanding.
> Take no notice of a loose woman,
> for the lips of this alien drip with honey,
> and her speech is smoother than oil;
> her ways wander, and she knows it not.
> Keep your way far from her,
> and do not go near the door of her house.

Although I have no intention of going near the door of her house, I have a moral obligation to denounce her behaviour. If standards are to be preserved in the community, judgement has to be passed on those who scorn right conduct. Wrongdoing has to be named for the destructive behaviour it is. We cannot force our critical judgement into early retirement in the name of an amorphous love which is indistinguishable from moral obtuseness. Love is not enough to keep people in the right bed, or to stop them from murdering their opponents. I love my wife, but it is the Law rather than my frail love that keeps me faithful to her. It is holy fear of the Law's conviction, not love, that keeps us all on the paths of righteousness. And it is the wisdom of the Law, not love, that educates the way we see people and act towards them.

In these trying circumstances, another small drink will not go amiss. Praise God, I always say, for the gift of the grape!

Perhaps Jesus' independence and restless travelling have left him unsympathetic to the accepted rituals of courtesy and propriety. Jesus is single, unattached to family, free from the normal daily obligations that tie one to a particular group of people and a particular place and a particular job. He is a free spirit, with no financial worries, supported as he is by women of means who follow him wherever he goes. Without his rich women, where would he be?

Does he realise that most people are exhausted trying to honour God, love their families, earn enough to feed and clothe them, and preserve whatever jobs they have in safekeeping? It is awesome to consider the amount of energy expended by ordinary people in securing what Jesus takes for granted: daily bread.

I suspect his itinerant style of life blinds him to the raw ordinariness of people's lives. Unlike the rest of us, he does not have to stay around and live with the consequences of what he says. It is easy to be romantic about tearful women when you do not have to live with them in the same community.

Jesus is free to walk away, drift at ease along the open road, enter this village or that town; in each new place he can meet credulous people, accept their invitations, eat their food and drink their wine, and wreck the decent calm which he calls stagnant. Then off he goes again on his bleak rounds, and the cycle repeats itself as if it has never happened before. If prophet he be, then his grim afflatus does little to encourage those of us who try to live a settled life worthy of our calling.

I believe the time is coming when people's hurt will

make them wise, as mine has surely done, and they will protect themselves and their families by refusing to receive him into their towns.

A final drink will surely do no harm, a deserved consolation before retiring to bed. I lean forward, lift the jug and tilt it into the waiting cup, but consolation there is none. The jug is empty. My cup is empty. All pleasure is spent. With nothing more to sip or savour, the time has come, I think, for bed.

As I lift myself from the couch, I can feel the joints in my knees protesting. I steady myself, turn and walk over to the open window. The night breeze feels cool and refreshing on my warm face. From where I stand I can see a dark sky embroidered with stars, with a waning moon as its centrepiece. Up there it all looks so ordered, so profound, so peaceful. I wonder what those far-flung lights think, if think they can, when they gaze down upon our unsorted world, our feasts that failed, our wanting that ends in hurting. Seeing everything while keeping everything at bay, does their distance from us make them wiser? Do our thin clarities disappoint them? Do they know they are admired even as they shine on our grief?

I turn away from the window and from my lunatic questions. Questions, always questions, stirring us to what? So many questions only lead to more questions. "Simon, do you see this woman?" Simon, I ask myself, do you see anything?

The room seems so much darker now, smaller somehow. I feel my way along the walls, to avoid falling over the couches, and gradually make it to the doorway. I know I am there when there is nothing more to feel. I pause and sniff the air, but it is difficult to tell if the atmosphere has returned to normal. By morning, certainly.

After a backward glance into the dark of the room, I

head across the courtyard for the dark of the stairs. I curse myself for not lighting a lamp. Why am I groping around in the dark? To save oil? Climbing the stairs feels like climbing Mount Hermon. I hug the stairs as I take each ponderous step. Not long to go, I think.

I wonder where the woman is now, where Jesus is. Are they in each other's dreams?

If only Jesus could see me now...

MARTHA

"**Y**ou should get out of the house more," Mary is saying. "It would do you a power of good. You never know who you might meet." When she says this, she nudges me.

I am drawn back to the conversation with my sister. I've been distracted watching a young mother, just a few paces ahead of us, talk away contentedly to her baby as our group returns from the market in Jerusalem. The baby, bundled in rough, brown cloth, is wide-eyed with delight as its mother makes up some nonsensical story. What a natural pair! I am suffused with longing. I can feel the old ache inside me, the craving to hug my own child to my heart, to be a mother to new life and new hope. Home-grown love. My baby, I decided, would be wrapped in cloth I had embroidered myself; my baby would always know it was only a blink away from love and security and me. And I would try to learn some funny stories, to shorten the journeys we would surely make together.

My sister's voice brings me back to the real world. I shift the weight on my back, the creel loaded with goods we've bought in the market, and smile at her. "But who'd look after Lazarus if I were gallivanting around the country?" I ask. "He's not getting any better and he needs someone to be there all the time. You know how he is."

"There's nobody with him now, and he'll still be the same when we get back. You fuss him too much, Martha."

I say nothing. Mary means well. Our brother Lazarus has been ill now for five years, gradually wasting away. He looks as thin as a stalk of wheat. In the early days we had a procession of doctors examine him, but we're none the wiser about what's wrong. We've given up on the doctors. I try my best. Every morning and evening I rub oil on his wasting body, to ease his sores and calm him; and I've tried all sorts of cures – rosemary, hyssop, rue, polygonum, even mandrake – but to no obvious good. I pray a lot for the poor soul, but I doubt he'll ever be his old self again. He never used to be cranky.

"Here, let me carry the creel for awhile," Mary offers. We are beginning to climb up the Mount of Olives to Bethphage.

"It's all right, Mary, I'm used to it now. Anyway it's too heavy for you."

"Please yourself, big sister, but don't say I didn't offer. Shout if you want any help." She moves up the line to talk to some of the other women.

Mary is good. Her goodness seems so natural that it looks effortless, like her way with people. I don't know what I would do without her. She keeps me alive. She loves life, and life loves her in return. She is also very beautiful, the first thing that strikes people when they see her. All the men in the market place turn their head when she passes, their eyes drinking her in. Even the Babylonian traders shine when she picks up the silk cloth she cannot possibly afford and strokes it with her fingers. Mary loves texture.

I stop for a moment and take a few deep breaths. I pull on the two ropes over my shoulders, to shift the creel higher up my back. The load is too heavy to carry on my head. It's my own fault, I tell myself. If I went to the market more often, my loads would be lighter.

When I do go to the market I want to do my business and get back home as quickly as possible. Mary enjoys lingering, looking, drawing attention to this and that. I always keep my eye out for false weights and for any bargains or special offers on the things we need. Mary sails past all this, shouting to me to look at this stunning necklace or smell this exotic scent. "Look at this!" she will cry as she picks up a gorget and tries it round her neck. "How do I look?" She has an eye for beauty and colour, especially for unusual things from faraway places. She takes me out of myself, I admit, and makes me pay attention to other worlds.

I worry that so many men seem to know her name. Some come to the house, many saying they're calling to see Lazarus, but it's Mary's smile and approval they are after. I've warned her about being too ready to talk to strangers, too charming to men, too eager to put herself forward. People might think her a bit flighty. But she shrugs off my warnings, saying that being charming to everyone is her protection. Perhaps she's right. I know she means no harm, but I worry all the same. She's only seventeen.

The climb to Bethphage on the heights of the Mount of Olives is steep and stony, and I have to watch every step I take. Up until recently I used to bring our donkey with me to the market. Poor old Josephine was a clumsy partner! On the way there she would be laden with goods we had to sell – olives, figs, woollen cloth – and on the way back she would carry whatever food and wool and essentials we needed. Every so often she would swerve suddenly as if to avoid something, but there was never anything there. Crazy! Other times you could spend more energy hauling her stubborn neck over ridges than you would carrying the stuff yourself.

She's getting on now, our Josephine, and she's too shaky on her legs to be trusted. How I miss her! These days she grazes on the slopes at the back of the house, free of shackles and packs. A retired donkey, if you please! She's too old to sell, but the village children love her and climb all over her. Funny how she's so patient with them.

By the time our little group reaches Bethphage it must be about the sixth hour. The weather is hot, the sun is high in a cloudless sky. There's no let up, not even the rumour of a breeze. I try to blink away the sweat running into my eyes. The load seems stuck to my back like a huge growth. I stagger to a halt, but not so much that you'd notice, and Mary helps me lower the load to the ground.

We all rest by the well and drink the cool water. I look around the group of women to see what the young mother and her baby are doing, but they are nowhere to be seen. When I ask Mary about them, she tells me their names, where they're from, which family they are visiting in Bethphage. Trust Mary to know!

As we sit in the shade, I feel exhausted and spent. I lean on my knees to stop them shaking. Mary keeps us cheerful as she chats away to everyone. I'm no great talker, mainly because I never know what to say to people. I always admire people who manage somehow to have lots to say and are never stuck for a word. After greeting people and telling them how Lazarus is, I dry up. I'm at a loss as usual. I suppose I should practise more, but Lazarus, like me, seems to prefer the quiet.

When we get our breath back, we move off again. This time we walk in single file, picking our way along the ridge and down the eastern slope to Bethany. The ridge is the most awkward part of the journey, where you have to be careful not to slip. If you do, and I have, you can cut yourself badly on the small jagged stones that stick out of the earth like spearheads. Mary tries to ease my load by lifting it from the back.

Our group makes it safely to the village, without any casualties. Mary and I wave goodbye to the others and head for the house, the last in the village. Beyond us there's no road.

When we reach home Josephine is sniffing and wheezing around the door. She looks up at us with those huge, brown, plaintive eyes. Look at me, she seems to be saying. The poor thing is probably thirsty. I pat her on the neck as I pass and tell her I'll fetch some water.

I hear voices from the room upstairs. Lazarus has a visitor.

"It's Jesus! " Mary shouts. And she runs upstairs to greet him.

Jesus is something of a regular at our house and it's always good to see him. He fits in like an extra brother. He feels at home here, not least because Bethany is something of a Galilean settlement. When you hear people talk in Jerusalem about "that hideout for foreigners," you know they mean Bethany. Which is probably why we attract more Roman patrols than any of the surrounding villages.

Jesus and Lazarus are best friends. They go way back. Lazarus was born in Nazareth and lived there until he was eleven. That's when my father, at the invitation of his elder brother, moved south for better work. He bought a small olive grove about a mile from here; it's on the western slopes of the Mount, a place called Gethsemane, which he and Lazarus worked for years. Both my parents are now dead, and since Lazarus fell ill Mary and I have worked the land.

Jesus has always kept in touch with Lazarus, more so since he began his work of preaching and healing up and down the country. When Jesus comes south with his disciples he always manages to slip away for a while and come here. He jokes that we are the only friends he has who aren't disciples. Lazarus always says that Jesus needs friends more than he needs disciples.

One thing puzzles me about their relationship. Jesus is a man of God who is graced with many gifts, among them the gift of healing. I remember a couple of years ago how he arrived distraught at the house, puzzled at the healing power that had suddenly emerged from nowhere. He kept saying, "If, if it is by the finger of God that I cast out evil, then the kingdom of God is really here." Lazarus kept assuring him that there was no if about it, that the finger of God really was at work. But puzzle me this: why does Jesus not heal Lazarus? If he loves my brother so much, how can he bear to watch him fade to nothing? Why doesn't Jesus touch Lazarus with the finger of God?

I say this, I confess, not only for the sake of Lazarus but for my own sake. I love my brother and I will look after him; but if Lazarus is healed, I am released, too. Both of us are set free. As long as he is bedridden I am tied to this place. Once, three years ago, I did meet someone who expressed an interest in me, a donkey-peddlar from Bethphage, a quiet man called Mark. But when I told him, as I had to, that I could never leave Lazarus while he was ill, or tie Mary down as my replacement, he said he couldn't be more sorry. He was polite and firm and final. Oh, Mark! If you only knew that my most treasured memory is the disappointment on your face as you turned away that day!

I suppose I'm afraid of ending up an old maid. I dread people forever saying, "There goes poor old Martha. She's so good and faithful. A credit to the family and an example to the rest of us." Can I tell you something? I'm tired of being a credit, tired of being forebearing, tired of being a woman whose price is above rubies. I'd like to unload some of the spiritual jewellery.

Sometimes, usually when I'm alone at night, I pray to God for the gift of a normal life. I have no grand designs for the future. What I want is what is normal. I want to carry babies in my arms as well as packs on my back. I want to be held as well as to hold. I want to invest my love and attention in growing life as well as in declining health. That's not so unusual, is it?

All this wishing isn't healthy. It can't amount to anything, can it?

I am still tidying everything away when Jesus and Mary come down. Jesus looks worn out. We kiss and exchange greetings. "Just look at you," I say to him. "If you get any thinner you'll look like Lazarus. When did you last eat?"

"It's good to see you again, Martha. I'm fine, really fine."

"How did you find our brother?"

"Tired. He's dozing off again. I think he wants to rest now."

"Sit down," Mary says. "You must tell us all your news. What have you been up to since we saw you last?" She takes Jesus by the hand and sits him down at table, and then settles herself at his feet.

I go outside to prepare something to eat. Our cooking-fire is just a hole in the ground, bordered by three stones, with a clay plate on top. I set the fire, light it, and put a bowl of water on to boil. Normally we eat very little at midday. The rabbis say that to eat at noon is to throw a stone into a wine-skin. But Jesus is our guest. Besides, he looks famished. I don't know what his women followers give him to eat. He looks as if they're on strike.

When the fire looks good I go back into the house, to get fish and vegetables from the food cupboard. Jesus is telling a story about a sower who throws seed all over the place, even in places where thorns and brambles grow. Sounds a dreadful waste to me, but I say nothing. He says something about those who hear the word of God, but how the word gets choked by all their worries and anxieties.

I take the food outside. Some of us have to worry, I think to myself. If you care, you worry. And if nobody else seems to care, you worry all the more. Sometimes you get choked up worrying about this or that. I wrap the fish in palm leaves and lay them on the clay plate, then start cutting the vegetables. Josephine sidles up to the fire to have a nose at what's cooking. I clap my hands and she moves away.

I go back inside. Mary is still sitting at the feet of Jesus. The table still needs to be laid. I am upset, but neither of them seems to notice. They're feeding on stories.

When I start setting the table I try giving Mary a meaningful look, but I might as well whistle for a Roman legion to recite the Shema. It isn't just being taken for granted that gets to me; I disapprove of Mary playing the part of the attentive disciple. In their wisdom rabbis don't have women disciples, or women pupils swooning at their words. It's not a woman's place to discuss the scripture or probe the inner workings of the word of God. Jesus should know better, unless he's becoming captivated by his beautiful disciple. Another reason for getting Mary on her feet.

I put the jug of wine on the table, then on impulse I blurt out, "Jesus, don't you care that my sister has left me to do all the serving by myself? Tell her to give me a hand."

Mary's cheeks go bright red, but she doesn't make to get up.

Jesus looks up and replies, "Martha, Martha, you worry about so many things, yet only one thing is needed. Mary has chosen the good part, which will not be taken from her."

I feel diminished. Wiped out. I feel like the resident idiot, the one who does, the one who gets written off in a clever line. It's like Jesus has passed judgement on me, forever. What can I say? Even if I could find the words, I can't find the breath.

Jesus and Mary are looking up at me, waiting for me to say something, or waiting for me to sit down. I stand there gawping as I pull on my apron strings. Pull yourself together, I tell myself, don't get melodramatic. I start nodding my head slowly, as if I understand what Jesus has said, and then I turn away before they can see the tears in my eyes. Best to leave them to it, I decide, and go look at the fish.

When I go outside it feels as if I've banged the door shut behind me, with the keys inside.

The meal is something of a disaster. The fish and vegetables turn out all right, the wine is cool and dry, the bread is fresh and soft, but the conversation is slow and restrained. We don't say much, but give most of our attention to the food. We're all on edge. I feel like an intruder. I have spoiled everything.

"This fish is special," Jesus says. "It must have come from Galilee." He smiles.

Mary says, "We wouldn't dream of buying fish that comes from anywhere else, would we Martha?"

"No," I say. I haven't a clue, of course, where the fish comes from. Can't say I care either. Fish is fish.

From somewhere outside comes the shout of children's voices calling for Josephine. The name gets repeated over and over again. A cry of delight goes up when she's discovered, then everything goes quiet again as the voices get fainter and fainter.

"I hope you like the vegetables," I say. "They are our own. Home-grown."

"They're great!" Mary exclaims. "And they're seasoned just right." She smacks her lips in approval. "If I could cook like Martha, every man in Judaea would be offering me his hand in marriage."

After this strange observation, we fall quiet again.

I pick up courage to apologise for my earlier outburst. I am still surprised at its suddenness and its tone. They smile their acceptance. They see my hurt. They are attentive and polite in a way they shouldn't have to be.

I spend most of the time moving the beans around my plate. Soon, I imagine, we'll be discussing the weather.

Jesus asks me how I'm feeling. I am about to tell him, spill my kept frustration on to the table, but when I look at Mary I can see her eyes beg me to keep my pain to myself. Hold back, hold back, she seems to be saying to me.

I say, "Fine, I'm really fine now. My back is a bit sore and my neck is a bit stiff from the journey from Jerusalem. That makes me irritable. But it's nothing a good lie-down won't cure."

Mary looks at me, relieved. Suddenly from upstairs comes the sound of a steady snore. Each of us smiles, grateful for the distraction.

"Have some more," I say as I pass the bowl of fish to them. "There's more of everything."

Jesus says, "Thanks, Martha, but I really can't eat any more."

"Me neither," Mary says. "That was delicious. A feast."

"You must be tired, Martha," Jesus says. He rises. "I'll leave you now so you can get some rest."

"You're not going already," I say.

"I'd better be getting back to the others. They'll think I've gone into hiding."

Mary and I rise together, and after Jesus says a prayer of thanksgiving we walk to the door to say our goodbyes. Jesus embraces both of us and thanks us for the company and the meal.

"Don't let it be so long before we see you again," Mary says.

"Say goodbye to Lazarus for me," Jesus says. "God keep you well."

He makes his way up the slope of the Mount towards Bethphage. Mary and I stand at the door and watch him in silence until he disappears over the rise. As I turn to go back inside, I can feel a breeze on my face. Somewhere out over the desert, a wind is beginning to pick up.

Remembering that dinner is like remembering a death, or some final loss that can never be redeemed. Last night I had a strange dream. I was having a picnic with Jesus and Mary. Lazarus was nowhere to be seen. The three of us were sitting on the edge of a precipice, our feet dangling in thin air. Jesus and Mary were dressed in their normal clothes, but I was wearing an old shift I throw on when I go to bed. Lying behind us was a huge pile of food, untouched. None of us was speaking; each of us was staring into the abyss. Then I woke up.

Neither Mary nor I ever refer to the visit of Jesus. We carry on as if nothing has happened, but we both know something has. Both of us have been to the edge. Both of us have backed away.

Jesus is right, of course. There's more to life than what I'm doing. Mary has chosen the better part and it will not be taken from her. It's all very well for Mary. She is free to choose, free to make time, free to sit and rise when she pleases. I'm not saying she's irresponsible, only that she's always protected herself from being tied down. She's a free spirit, and nobody will take that away from her. All the same, I would hate to lose her, either to marriage or discipleship. It's only a matter of time before she leaves this place, and when she does I shall miss her more than life itself.

As for Lazarus and me, what shall become of us? In another five years will I still be feeding him, washing him, turning him, oiling him, exercising him, keeping the schedule of care? If that is what is needed, that is what I will do. I will wait for him, and I will love him until death steals him away; and then, if it is not too late, I'll try to build my own life.

Five years ago, when Lazarus fell ill, I remember saying to him, "Don't worry about anything, brother dear. I'll look after you and do your work in the fields. You rest and get better. For the time being I will mind everything." Like everyone else, I believed this state of affairs was temporary, so every decision I made was provisional. Everything in life was for the time being. Things would change, for sure.

Things haven't changed. Not yet. But what of tomorrow? Tomorrow will be another day the same. Tomorrow I will get up early, set the fire, bake the day's bread and prepare a light meal for Lazarus and Mary.

When Lazarus has eaten, I will wash him and oil him and turn him and rub his aches. He will ask me how I am, what's new, what's to be done in the fields. I'll tell him I'm fine, that there's no great news, that Gethsemane is looking good but the other fields need attention.

When Mary rises we will decide who will go to the fields and who will stay at home to make the woollen cloth and keep an eye on Lazarus. Whatever we decide, both of us will work hard through the day.

Then evening will come, much like any other evening. The meal will be made and served, and later, after everything is cleared, Lazarus will be rubbed and settled for the night. Josephine will pick her way down the hill and stand outside the house, hoping to be thrown some tasty leftovers. Someone might call to visit Lazarus or Mary, or me, and we will talk a while. If there is light to work by, I might do a bit of embroidery.

I will light the oil lamps, the shadows on the walls will move and dance like a lost child, and thoughts will crowd in on me. I will sit in the corner until the guttering flames die into darkness, and the remains of another day are gathered and traded for another tomorrow.

Somewhere else, out under the stars and around a generous fire, Jesus will be telling new stories to his chosen disciples, throwing words generously into the dark, words that will make a difference to someone's tomorrow.

Where does time go to? What happens to time when it seeps away from us? Is there some vast secret place where lost time is stored, where some kind guardian spirit lives who'll give us back the time that's vanished on us, the time due us? But if I could reclaim the time I've lost, what would I do with it? Could it turn out that all I had left was time?

Morbid thoughts, these. Whenever I get around to thinking about things, the results are always disastrous.

"Martha, Martha, you worry about so many things...."

You bet.

A SECRET
AGENT

My name is unimportant. As a secret agent I am always reluctant to sign anything, preferring to give my reports by word of mouth. I am writing these thoughts to no one in particular; I am addressing an imaginary "you" to whom I can tell as much of the truth as I conveniently can. There is no one else I would trust.

One day last year I was approached by an official from the high priest's palace. I was leaving the house of a Jerusalem elder – where I had spent the morning teaching Greek and Latin composition to several children – when the official introduced himself and asked if he might walk with me for awhile. He said that he knew my father from the meetings of the Sanhedrin. "However," he said, "I would be obliged if you didn't mention our little meeting to him. You know how it is."

As we walked he spoke about the importance of security and how good intelligence work was essential to the maintenance of law and order. He offered me a job that could, he said, play a part in determining the future of our nation.

He seemed to know a great deal about me, and gave me the impression that I had been selected by some council too secret to be named, for some task too important to be declined.

"If you agree to become an intelligence officer," he said, "you will simply have to keep us informed about one or two people and what they get up to – that sort of thing. This may involve some risk to yourself, but I have always found that danger has its own rewards. You will be paid generously and will benefit from the experience and expertise of your colleagues in the profession. Of course, if you prefer to stay with your teaching career, we will understand. Perfectly. But we would like your answer now. You will not be asked again."

I said yes, trying not to appear too grateful. He said they had something of an entrance examination for me: I was to draft a report on someone called Nicodemus, a member of the Sanhedrin. Nicodemus, he insisted, was not under any suspicion; but he would serve as a soft target for my first assignment. My report would be picked up by messenger in two weeks' time.

They must have been pleased with my work, for three days after my report was collected I received an invitation to meet Caiaphas himself. I was flattered. I was in.

The high priest was urbane, witty and charming – the kind of man who gives you the impression that he is privileged to meet you. He congratulated me on my report, then went on to stress that my abilities were not as important as my obedience to him. Obedience would be the test of my true vocation. I had been chosen, he explained, to monitor Jesus of Nazareth, who was becoming something of a worry to the religious authorities.

My employer gave me this advice: "Aim yourself towards your target's conviction. Follow him, listen to him; note who follows him and who is obliged to him; discover what he is afraid of, and why. No information about him is irrelevant. But do not be distracted by what he says: watch what he actually does. Whatever you do, you must never get yourself noticed. Take part in nothing; never draw attention to yourself; make the background your natural habitat. Others have been appointed to ask questions; you must not. If we ever feel the need to bring Jesus to trial, your intelligence will serve the basis of our case. You are our eyes and our ears, and we are confident that you will not disappoint us. You are to send your reports only to me. Go now in peace."

That is how it all started.

Let me be frank with you. I joined the ranks of spies in the hope that I could escape from the unrelieved boredom of my life. Real life troubled me; I was an up-and-coming mistake; the future held no secret. I became a runaway, restless for adventure and hungry for the power to reorder the world to my own liking.

Before I became a secret agent, I imagined I would be joining the elite corps of intelligent and imaginative professionals, a company of trained experts equipped to face danger with still more dangerous skills. A priestly caste, I thought, whose real importance could never be truly measured. I fancied that their commitment and boldness of spirit would somehow rub off on me and that eventually I would become a man of consequence and discover the hero within myself.

What I ended up joining was a shabby collection of drunkards, whores and inadequates, an assembly of those who had been defeated by reality, a rag-bag assortment of people with leftover lives and nowhere to go but sponsored fantasy. Most of them are insecure fools, vain enough to imagine that the undercover world will give them the kind of respectability that the real world has so firmly denied them. They have all been booby-trapped by reality, and they have organised their own recovery by creating a world in which they can muddle through and which nurtures their silly conceits.

They should all go away and do something honest – like digging roads.

If they experience the tension generated by deception, you could not tell by listening to them or watching them. Whatever real identity they ever had, they have lost touch with it – just as they have lost touch with the instinct for truth. Every profession has its own definition of truth. For the secret agent, truth has become a useful fiction: you lure the facts towards it until everything fits tidily into its appointed place.

Don't misunderstand me. I am no different from them. I am one of them and I am wary of them. We all play a part, even to each other. I know that they will never disclose themselves to me, just as I will never disclose myself to them. We have to settle for cover.

Our job is anything but adventurous. We inform on people; we rob them of their privacy; we report their enthusiasms with disapproval; we draw our wages from their passions. We are impotent dwarfs who strut around despising other people's struggles in love – while all the time disguising our inner emptiness with practised smiles. We have an allegiance to nothing. We savour nothing. And we have nothing in ourselves to betray.

You may ask why I stay if I am so disenchanted with my lot. That is a question that awakens me every morning and I have no satisfactory answer. I suppose I stay because I cannot leave; I have no other world to go to. My skills of deception are not easily marketable – except to the Romans. But to become their secret agent now would be to throw away my life, such as it is. If I crossed over to them, my old compatriots would surely catch up with me and relieve me of the burden of ever having to answer another question.

The principal reason for my disaffection is Jesus himself. In a strange way I have come to respect him, even though I know that I will never figure him out. I admire his nerve. He is his own man, a dangerous one, and looks to no one for approval. He has a great love for ordinary people, educating them to be suspicious of any authority which lords it over them and which uses them to subsidise its own comic importance. He has a profound respect for everyone's private struggles and a keen disrespect for those who refuse to take people's weakness and pain into account.

He keeps on the move, never staying long in the one place. He has neither wife nor children. If he had any friends in his youth, they are nowhere to be seen now. He is detached, but not aloof. I find it strange, however, that he does not belong to any party or sect: this makes it very difficult to classify his beliefs. He seems to have no desire for the priesthood – which is just as well, since the sabbath laws have so little hold on him. In all my time with him I have never heard him utter a single word in favour of the religious authorities. In that sense, he does not appear particularly religious and I have never seen him engage in any cultic act.

He is a very public person, which appears to make him an easy target. However, no self-respecting person could approve of the company he keeps – a real circus of the crooked and the cracked, who look to him for affection and support. If anyone can actually enjoy the company of these weirdos, Jesus can. He has dinner parties for them, and they return the favour by turning up uninvited at formal dinners where he is a guest of honour. Jesus finds all this amusing and he tells his shocked hosts that they should *organise* their dinner parties like this.

He has a subversive sense of humour.

Not surprisingly, the people who have the highest

regard for him are the sick. I am no expert on the matter, but I would say that they love him. They come to him in droves, they limp to him, they feel their way to him, they crawl to him, they are carried to him. An emergency-ward on the move, driven by the hope that he will free them at last from the weight of their suffering.

I have watched them in amazement. A blind man slowly feels the face of Jesus, as if he is fingering the features of God. A deaf-mute follows the shape of Jesus' lips, hoping that he will see a word that will cure him. A father and mother, crazed with worry, carry the twitching body of their child and hold it before him like some broken promise. A few cripples, too shy or too tired to push themselves to the front, wait as they have waited all their lives – at the edge of the gathering.

I wait with them.

It is important that I don't meet Jesus personally, although this is becoming harder to manage the closer I follow him. Sometimes the crowds he addresses are small, making concealment difficult. Recently Jesus has taken to nodding to me as if acknowledging my attentive presence, a practice that is as puzzling as it is disconcerting. To avoid him at dinner gatherings involves me in a display of gymnastics that is quite exhausting. He is certainly aware of my footwork. Does he know why I follow him? If he does, why doesn't he say something?

I have received instructions from Caiaphas to make a special report on Jesus' practice of welcoming sinners to his house in Capernaum. The high priest is aware how much this disturbs the Pharisees and the scribes: if he can make capital out of their cultural and theological sensibilities, he might secure their collaboration in managing Jesus' eventual downfall.

The Pharisees and scribes are strict in limiting table fellowship to a circle of approved religious people. They make no objection when Jesus feeds needy sinners, but they cannot tolerate his habit of receiving them as guests and eating with them. In our society, as in many others, sharing a meal with others is a serious matter which has profound religious significance. To break bread with others is to accept them, to offer them brotherhood and forgiveness, to honour them, to make a sanctuary for them, to share life with them. Curiously, it is *because* Jesus believes all this that he welcomes sinners and eats with them. The way he includes sinners in table fellowship has become the strongest sign of the message he preaches and, for my part, the most compelling proof of his strange integrity.

For a time I could see little purpose in these gatherings, but gradually I began to understand them as Jesus' peculiar way of bringing people to conversion. His method is built on respect rather than threat: in associating with sinners through table fellowship, Jesus is clearly affirming their basic worth – which is why the Pharisees and scribes object so strongly. Jesus does not believe that making people feel like moral lepers is likely to lead to repentance; it is more likely, he claims, to lead to moral paralysis. Nor does he believe that summing up people by their wrongdoing, thus isolating them in guilt, forms a secure foundation for spiritual renewal. Categorical decisions prompted only by feelings of guilt are as fragile as their foundation. New life, he insists, needs more than the memory of guilt if it is to flourish. (I must confess, though I cannot include this in my report, that Jesus might be right on this one.)

I have attended a number of these meals, all prepared by women followers of Jesus who never seem short of a denarius or two. I'm not sure how the teacher manages to do it, but somehow he creates an atmosphere in which people seem to breathe more easily, as if relieved from the sour knowledge that no matter what they say they will never be accepted anyway. I have seen how people's defences are gradually lowered before the realisation that Jesus approaches them from the standpoint of friendship, accepting them, forgiving them, hoping in them. His guests discover themselves speaking without lying, saying what they feel, naming their pain and failure and fantasy.

Often he says very little, content to encourage someone to speak, letting the other listeners say how the speaker's condition might reflect their own.

Sometimes Jesus tells a story to catch something of the mystery and reality of God. Usually this is a parable about a genial host who throws a magnificent banquet for a crowd of important people, all of whom promise to come. But when the oxen are roasted and everything is ready, the serious guests have other things more important than keeping their festal appointment. The host is hurt and angry, but he refuses to cancel the party; instead, he takes to the streets and the alleyways to invite the poor and the maimed and the homeless, assuring them this is no trick: his parties are for real. When suspicions have been allayed, a solemn procession of misfits makes its way to the promise of party. They shuffle into the great hall to the cheers of the waiting servants, who welcome them with a kiss of greeting, anoint their heads with the oil of gladness, and wash their feet with care. When the bewildered guests become accustomed to the light of so many candles, they see the waiting banquet and commit themselves to do serious damage to the array of food decorating the tables. This is a chance of a lifetime, this is a chance of life. When every place is filled, the blessing is proclaimed, the bread is broken, the wine is poured, and the party has no choice but to begin. And in the midst of all the flushed faces and the laughter there sits the eccentric host delighting in the company that graces his table.

From the way I have seen Jesus treat sinners and from the stories of God I have heard him tell, I would say that his most radical value is this: that sinners can begin to change their mind about themselves and others and God when they are open to the acceptance and forgiveness that table fellowship with Jesus offers them. If I understand Jesus correctly, he acts on the belief that true conversion follows after table fellowship. This appears scandalous to so many righteous people, but the teacher quotes the tradition of Wisdom on God's forbearance:

> You are merciful to all, because you can do all things; you overlook men's sins so that they can repent.

Traditional religious authorities observe the reverse sequence: sinners are forgiven only after repentance has been exacted. For most religions, forgiveness is conditional. For Jesus, forgiveness is unconditional, it is sheer gift, freely given. It is not a reward for repentance because, like mercy, it reflects the generosity of the one who gives, not the worthiness of the one who receives. Nobody deserves mercy, Jesus says; it would not be mercy if they deserved it.

Jesus insists that it is human forgiveness, not God's, that is at the heart of his disagreement with the Pharisees and scribes. God's forgiveness is never at issue. He is a professional forgiver; his track record is flawless, not least because everyone gives him endless opportunities for exercise. The problem is not whether God forgives; the problem is whether his creatures do. Jesus' argument is simple: God forgives us readily, so we should forgive each other in the same way.

Even Jesus' own disciples have trouble grasping this teaching, because they believe that there must be some condition, some final arithmetic to the business of forgiveness. Jesus says no. Seventy-times seven. Forgiveness without end.

Which is why he continues to welcome sinners and eat with them.

I have been puzzling how to write my special report on Jesus as an indiscriminate host. Caiaphas is not interested in my evaluation of Jesus' ministry – I am no theologian; he claims interest only in accurate reporting of what Jesus does and says. No doubt the high priest has others to assess the information that crosses his desk. As for the accuracy of my reporting: that will doubtless be hijacked to serve a case against Jesus.

From my own contacts in Jerusalem I know that Caiaphas is preparing a list of charges against Jesus: blasphemy, treason, subverting religious authority, perverting sacred tradition, being soft on sin. The menu is awesome. Caiaphas is my paymaster, but I feel no loyalty to him, in spite of how he rattles on about the principal virtue of obedience to him. Anyone who places loyalty to his person above loyalty to the truth displays a moral nervousness that can be easily exploited. The high priest may be cunning, but he is afraid of Jesus and alarmed at his power over the common people. The majority of his colleagues feel the same. The fear and alarm of the religious authorities will turn out to be the hidden but resolute witnesses in the case against Jesus.

I have no personal investment in seeing Jesus imprisoned and put down, though I believe this will surely come to pass. Jesus has no serious talent for survival, even though he has shown that he can make himself scarce when the opposition tightens its grip around him. They will not endure him in the south, least of all in Jerusalem; he has a small chance of seeing old age if he stays among his own people in Galilee, who have an inherited tolerance for religious difference and ambiguity. If Jesus journeys south, he will be heading for an appointment with the executioners. It is fixed. His last hours have already been written in the stars.

I wish it could be otherwise. I know him well enough to be sure that he will choose not to avoid the suffering that emerges from commitment to his values. The avoidance of suffering is not his governing passion; love is. That love will be the death of him.

That is why I believe that portraying Jesus sympathetically in my report will be a useless exercise. Nothing I can say or do will make any difference. I shall write my report as cautiously as I can, while I hug to myself the shameful secret of my admiration for Jesus.

There is one final thing I feel I have to say, though I don't know why I feel compelled to say it. The aristocratic high priest for whom I work would never eat with the likes of me; the prophet from Nazareth whom I am payed to spy on would eat with me anytime.

That has to mean something.

THE
ADULTERESS

We thought we were safe. Like many unlicensed lovers, we were absorbed in our new world, believing the real world was going about its business with a distracted air. We really thought we were fooling everyone and that no one could stumble on our unlikely alliance. We congratulated ourselves on our discretion, we drank to our new skills in deception. For sure, we were safe.

My lover was a young widower whose wife had died before giving birth to their firstborn. I might as well have been widowed too, for all the difference it made. At least I would have known where my husband was lying each night. I had been faithful to the man who claimed my virginity in marriage and then gave it back to me when he grew tired of me. He spent his energy elsewhere.

We were childless, an affliction that brought shame on both of us. His family were puzzled why he didn't divorce me, but children would have interfered with his outside interests. I was a useful cover. When he began staying away from home some nights, at first he used to mutter forced excuses for his absences and then give me a small gift the following day, to cover my grievance. It wasn't long before he was sold out of excuses and gifts. Our marriage had become an established fiction.

It was easier than I thought to slide into an affair. I

met the young widower at a wedding. He had a lost look about him, as if he had forgotten the reason why he had turned up at this party. I looked at him and he looked at me. I looked away. When I looked back at him, he was still looking at me. We smiled. Gradually we moved towards one another. We introduced ourselves. Easy.

That evening we met at his house. That night we untethered each other's long abstinence.

In the morning there were no murmurs of remorse or apology, no avoiding each other's eyes, no hastening away. There was no regret, no sorrow, no morning grief. We both delighted in the forgotten truth of our bodies, in the tenderness we had shared, in the prospect of doing it again and again. The affair had begun.

Don't misunderstand me. I'm not trying to justify it, but I see no reason to deny how it helped me. What I did was morally wrong. That I accept. However, I refuse to say our affair was shabby when it had its own awkward beauty; I refuse to say it was just a collusion of bodies when it gave me, for however brief a time, a taste of being longed for again and loved. You see I believed that love's mysterious power would never again connect me with another person, that it had passed me by forever. Then the affair started. For me, clandestine love was much less humiliating than conjugal loneliness. Of course it wasn't perfect. But believe me, I was grateful. I felt lucky. And I felt safe.

We were caught in the act. In the very act. My young widower surprised even me with the speed of his exit as he disappeared in a cloud of instant regret, grabbing his shirt and cloak, and shouting an apology over his shoulder. A classic case of bye-bye baby and amen. I was left lying on the bed as if I had been whiling away the time playing solitaire in the nude. There was no emergency exit for me. I was left to shoulder the blame and face the panorama of my accusers as they gathered around the bed. They stood gaping at me with the kind of faces that light up when they discover a new victim. Me.

They came closer. I was swooped down on, pitchforked out of bed, snatched up, thrown in a corner, ordered to cover my filthy body, then hauled out of the house by two moral enthusiasts.

My husband had carefully planned the arrest by selecting a group of his cronies to witness my infidelity. Clearly, he didn't believe mutual infidelity was a real option in our relationship. His infidelity was supposed to be met with my understanding. My infidelity was met with his solicitude for revenge. Now that I had been caught sinning, I was supposed to believe that it was the fulfilment of the Law he was after, not my blood. Some hope. He knew that all this would lead to my death, just as I knew that only my death would satisfy his hurt manhood.

All my accusers were men. All were religious men, scribes and Pharisees. That didn't cheer me up any, for I was unable to spot the difference between their religious zeal and the impatience of a lynch mob as they paraded me through the streets to the Temple. No one we passed on the way was left in any doubt about the moral purpose of this crusade. My husband was pointed out as the offended party; there was no need to point me out as the culprit. I was jeered at, spat upon, a soft target for everyone's derision. For the onlookers, it must have been good street theatre, with no one needing to puzzle out the real plot. By the time we reached the place where Jesus was teaching, we had attracted a procession of the curious, all eager to see what would happen to me.

Jesus was sitting in the middle of a small gathering in the Temple precincts, but whatever he was teaching was interrupted by our noisy arrival. My accusers pushed me forward and stood me in front of the teacher, then formed a circle around the two of us. The others gathered behind them. One man called his friends to come over beside him, to get a better view of the proceedings. Two street dogs were chased away. I didn't have the nerve to look at Jesus, who was sitting at my feet. I started to pray that he wouldn't discover he had an appointment elsewhere and excuse himself while he still had time.

One of my husband's friends, a lawyer noted for his pronouncements on matters of discipline, quoted the Law of Moses which stated that my decreed fate was to be stoned to death. As he developed the point, he made it clear to everyone within earshot that the execution of the Law meant the execution of me.

He was eloquent. The more I listened to him, the more I felt drawn into his line of argument. Jesus looked up at me, then with a gesture of his hand he invited me to sit beside him. He was going to sit it out. I was relieved that for once in my life my prayer had been answered. This man was not going to leave me in a heap of pain.

The lawyer was in full flow addressing his captive audience. He said, "It is impossible to overplay the value of the Law in our community. We are a people whose history defines who we are today and who we will be tomorrow. Our history was no accident; it was inevitable. Our history reveals the Law. Our history is the Law. If we are to be true to our fathers and true to ourselves, we must be true to the Law. Our great past is a direct legacy to us, and the future of our people will depend on the legacy we leave our children. The Law is impotent without our observance, and if we leave our children a Law that we ourselves disregard then we leave them a heritage and a destiny that is covered in dust. All the suffering, all the obstinate courage, all the fierce allegiance to the covenant will have been for nothing. For nothing.

"The continuation of our religion depends on the vitality of the Law. Through the Law we come to distinguish between good and evil, we come to the knowledge of the truth. And when we do evil, the Law convicts us of our wrongdoing and delivers a sentence of punishment. We need the Law to define the limits of what is acceptable behaviour. And some of us have the heavy responsibility to see that the Law is interpreted, obeyed, and enforced.

"Our responsibility to this woman is subsumed under the larger responsibility to the Law. Because of who she is and because of who we are, all of us are subject to the Law. That is our faith. That is our very identity. The Law itself clearly convicts this woman to the sentence of death by stoning.

"Some of you may talk of the need to be compassionate, but we should guard ourselves against appealing to compassion when we should be addressing the disgrace of sin. And never let us lose sight of the serious sin that is before us. Compassion is an important virtue; sensibility to the pain of others is a mark of the good life. The innocent should always be able to look to us for good example, as the weak should depend on our good guidance. But that guidance must itself be instructed by the Law. To claim to be compassionate while dishonouring the Law is a religious pretension that cannot be condoned. We must never allow our compassion to gainsay the explicit precepts of the Law. Never.

"If we permit this adulterous woman to live, we will be guilty of a greater crime than she has committed: we will be responsible for wiping out the Law itself. Indeed we will be responsible for murdering our own identity as the people of the Torah."

You may find this difficult to believe, but I couldn't help being impressed by the lawyer's performance, the forcefulness of his argument, his command of language, his unswerving authority. Needless to say, his conclusion terrified me; but he was probably a man of integrity whose sole cause in life was the defence of the Law.

The lawyer looked around the circle of the crowd. They were silent, impressed, expectant. Then he walked over to Jesus, who had been listening very attentively. The lawyer asked Jesus, "What do you have to say?"

Jesus looked up at the lawyer, then looked at me. I looked at the ground. Then Jesus bent forward and started doodling on the ground with his finger. The lawyer returned to his place among the witnesses.

The crowd was looking at Jesus, waiting for him to speak. I was going out of my mind, desperate for him to say something. There was no point in me saying anything, much less submit to the vulgarity of pleading for my life.

More doodles.

The other witnesses then started to give evidence against me. Their evidence could not have been more damning, but their malice showed through too clearly. They were not as controlled as the lawyer, and Jesus did not appear to be overwhelmed by their keen sense of moral duty. He wasn't fooled by all their anxious spouting, as if *their* lives depended on it. Nor, I'm sure, was he impressed by their division between man and woman, righteous and sinner, executioner and victim.

They might have guessed that, being who he was, he would be on the side of the victim. He was their victim, too. We shared that.

When the witnesses saw that Jesus was still not responding to their testimony, they changed their tactics and started to huff and puff about the sacredness of the Law; but that argument seemed to arrive too late after they had shown how much they hated me. They defied Jesus to make a judgement. They hoped to trap him. I knew that they wanted him more than me. He was in the middle, too. They probably reckoned on killing two birds with one stone.

As they persisted with their question, Jesus stood up and faced them. Silence. Slowly he began to walk around the circle of my accusers, starting with the lawyer, looking at each in turn, not missing one of them. He paused in front of my husband. Neither of them said a word.

Jesus then returned to his place beside me. As he stood there, all of us waited for him to pronounce his own judgement. He shrugged his shoulders, pointed at me, and issued his challenge, "Let the one among you who is without sin be the first to throw a stone at her." He sat down again beside me and continued doodling on the ground.

Whatever came to pass, Jesus was not going to join the moral majority.

No one moved. No one spoke. Silence. It was as if Jesus' challenge had returned them not to the written Law but to the unfinished chronicle of their own sins, the pathetic details of their own scripture. In a strange way I felt something like pity for them: pity for lives so crushed by the need to hurt, the need to inflict pain, the need to make someone pay for the whole rotten mess we get ourselves into. I knew that I was not the real target. But I knew I would do, for the time being.

Suddenly a small boy appeared from nowhere and

stood in the circle, looking around at all of us, his huge eyes unblinking, his mouth wide open. No one seemed to know him; no one called his name. After he had finished his inspection, he put his thumb in his mouth, toddled unsteadily through the crowd, then headed out of the precincts.

People began to fidget and to glance around, embarrassed by the quiet. They had come here to accuse, not to be accused. Those whose hands were free found themselves wanting some activity. Beards were fingered, cloaks were straightened, ears were rubbed, belts were tied in a tighter knot. Some Pharisees adjusted the phylacteries on their heads and arms. I could see some men looking to the lawyer who had spoken so eloquently, clearly hoping that he would give a new lead and save the day. But he seemed to have gone into a secret sanctuary within himself, to find his own answer to a question that troubled him.

A look of resignation appeared on the faces of many of my accusers. But how long would this remission last? The principal witnesses had the right to throw the first stones. I dared to look over to my husband but I could catch nothing from his face that gave me any hope. I closed my eyes and braced my body for slaughter.

Instinctively, I fell on my side and curled up into a tight ball; my knees cradled my head, which I protected with my hands. I wondered how they would do it. Would they stone me here? Or would they drag me to one of the city gates, throw me down backwards from the wall, and then stone me? The first stone was supposed to be aimed at the heart, but I had my heart well covered. I could hear the hammer of my own heart-beats and feel the tiny trembling of my whole body. The only other thing I could hear was the sound of Jesus' finger tracing shapes on the ground.

Then I heard a new sound, a series of dull thuds, which became louder and louder as stones began dropping from hands to earth. I tell you that you could hear it on the far side of eternity and it was the sweetest music I have ever heard. No words were spoken. There was just the shuffle of feet as people gradually moved away. It sounded like the grudging departure of mourners leaving a burial ceremony, each weighed down by a new solitude.

I waited for what seemed an age. And when I unfurled myself and looked up, all my accusers were gone. Including my husband. They had left me alone with Jesus. I sat up. When I looked across at Jesus I could see he was sweating. He wiped his brow with the sleeve of his cloak, then shook his head from side to side in silent disbelief. He had the look of a man who had just come to realise how near he had been to the precipice.

When Jesus turned to speak to me for the first time, I expected a list of probing questions and a sharp denunciation. But he did not dote on my sin. Neither did he ignore it. He asked me, "Woman, where are they? Has no one condemned you?"

I looked around again. "No one, sir," I replied.

"Neither do I condemn you," Jesus said. "Go your way and sin no more."

That is how I escaped with my life. Who could have imagined such unexpected mercy? I felt so happy, so free, so very lucky. It was as if someone had reached inside me, into my faltering heart, and let me have another chance, another go at life. I couldn't speak. I rose, turned, walked out of the precincts. When I looked back at Jesus, he was still sitting on the ground, alone, still doodling.

All that happened a month ago. Since then, my life seems empty somehow. As for the scribes and the

Pharisees, I know they will never forgive me. How can they? I am their bad news. Every time I pass them in the street, I remind them of him and their humiliation, I summon up whatever secret reasons shamed them into leaving me alone. And, believe me, I am alone. They robbed me of my lover; Jesus robbed them of their stones. But answer me this: who wins from all this?

I love Jesus for what he did for me. I escaped from my executioners, but what have I escaped into? How can I conjure a future out of my hopeless freedom? I am afraid. I don't want to disappoint Jesus, but neither do I want to spend the rest of my days with my sexual longings in protective custody. I am a woman, the kind of woman that needs bodily warmth as well as spiritual direction, the kind of woman that aches for tangible love, a love that cannot be satisfied by the consolation of a virtuous, solitary life. I'm sorry, but that's me.

Let me be frank with you. I am a bad investment for Jesus. He should have risked his reputation on a safer bet, on someone who had the strength to sin no more. If he had any idea how feeble I really am, would he have bothered to take my side? Would he have risked the certain revenge of religious men for the uncertain virtue of a fallen woman? I doubt that even Jesus is that foolish.

Life is rarely simple. Goodness is rarely uncomplicated. Mercy can be unnerving, not least because it makes expectations of you. Release from certain death can be frightening, really scary, because what you are released into might appear to be a different kind of death. I don't mean to sound ungrateful; it's just that I know myself well enough to be wary of what I can actually manage.

At the moment, I feel confused and unsure. It's difficult to explain. I feel like a widowed sleepwalker staggering among shadows, relearning the neuter touch of night.

The nights are lonely: so many unwanted hours. In the mornings, I get up late, to delay the onset of interminable days. I try to keep my waking hours crowded with things to do. Anything, to keep panic at bay. How long I can last like this is a mystery to me.

What hasn't diminished, in spite of my confusion, is my love for Jesus and respect for his courage. I have sort of escaped, but I doubt he will escape at all. He is a marked man; he will be the one to pay for all the mess we get ourselves into. He is the real victim. If they ever catch up with him, and they surely will, I pray that someone will come to his rescue and save him from his executioners. If not, he will end up exposed, naked, helpless. Solitaire.

A DISILLUSIONED DISCIPLE

At the outset I have to declare myself a lapsed supporter of Jesus of Nazareth. I have moved from enthusiasm through disillusionment to anger, and now I feel compelled to say why I can no longer believe in him. In accusing Jesus I am not aiming to destroy him; rather, I hope to spare others the disappointment and grief they will surely feel if, like me, they begin to place their hopes in him.

When I first encountered Jesus – it was during his first visit to our town – I became an immediate convert. The whole of Capernaum came alive during that visit; people talked about little else in their homes, in the market-place, at work. Never had we heard anyone speak with such authority, relate to people with such tenderness, reach out to the suffering with such individual attention.

My hopes were engaged immediately: maybe he was the prophet like Moses we had been waiting for; maybe he would lead us out of oppression and solitude and sorrow. It was so easy to hope in him. He was nothing like anything or anyone we had seen before. Compared with the scribes, he was like a priceless pearl among broken glass.

I was so overcome by Jesus and enthusiastic about what he was doing that I told my wife I had to leave home for a short while, to be free to follow this new prophet. She was appalled.

"Are you mad, Shamma?" she asked. "A stranger comes to town, tells a few stories in the synagogue, heals a few demented souls, and you want to run off with him! For God's sake, what for?"

"I think he might be the one we've been waiting for?"

"Who's we? I've got the man I've been waiting for, Shamma, and now he's running out on me."

"I'm not running out on you," I said. "It's just something I have to do."

"What about me? You know I'm pregnant with our first child. Anything could happen. You should be around. Why go chasing after a gypsy storyteller you know nothing about and leave your own family in the lurch?"

I didn't say anything.

"Has he asked you to go with him?"

"No," I said.

She started untying the huge knot at the end of her shawl.

"Have you told your parents?" she asked.

"No," I said. "I thought you might..."

"Great!" she shouted, throwing up her hands. "The adventurer disappears in a cloud of dust and leaves me to explain to the abandoned why he's gone. What about your work? You can't just turn your back on that. What's going to happen to all the shoes and sandals waiting to be made and mended? And what are we going to live on? Parables?"

"The work can wait awhile," I said. "I won't be away for long. There's enough money in our savings. You can use that."

"And when I run out of savings, what then?"

"You won't. Don't worry, I'll be back long before then. Look, I don't want this thing to come between us."

"Then don't go."

"I have to go," I said.

She looked at me. She started to pull her shawl until it looked she would tear it from her shoulders. Her hands were shaking, her knuckles were white.

I reached out to touch her, but she stepped backwards.

I turned away from her and left home.

For the next three months I followed Jesus from village to village. I listened to him speak, I watched how he related to the people who came to him for help. Wherever he went, his twelve companions went too. The two brothers Simon and Andrew I know well and respect – I have fitted them with sandals, they have provided our house with fish aplenty. One day Andrew offered to introduce me to Jesus, but I declined. By that time I was thinking my enterprise was a mistake and that it was already too late.

The very thing that first attracted me to Jesus became the first source of annoyance and disappointment.

You know that the most common preoccupation among our people, as among all poor rural communities, is sickness. Because our biggest worry is illness and disease, our prayers and pilgrimages are nearly always directed to the goal of physical health. This explains why the healers have always been the most sought after gurus in our society. Many of them are saints and mystics revered for holiness, some of them are charlatans who use other people's desperation to answer their own sick needs.

Jesus has an extraordinary gift of healing, which makes him hugely attractive to the crowds. Wherever he goes, the crowds follow him. He seems happiest when he is in their company. They feed each other. They need each other.

Jesus is drawn to intermittent people who are weak

and distraught, all those for whom religion is not a Temple of worshippers but a shelter for broken people. You must have noticed that Jesus only associates with those who are sick, sinful, mad, possessed, dumb, wretched, tormented, stupid. Although he shares none of these disabilities, he seems insecure around normal healthy people. Like many healers, he likes being a gladiator in an arena of wounded victims. And if, perchance, like some of the local scribes I know, you have clawed your way out of poverty or illiteracy or despair and take some pride in your achievement, then look out. Jesus' disapproval will land on you like a Herodian stone.

He has that villager's resentment against anyone who betters himself and moves beyond the range of local approval. Curiously he accuses his own people of convicting him in the same way, for they found it difficult to credit that a backwoodsman could become a national prophet. He has a similar problem. He is, for sure, a son of Nazareth.

When Jesus went to his home place he failed hopelessly with his own people. His failure was quickly interpreted as their obtuseness, but the Nazarenes were not entirely to blame. In his nervousness and anger Jesus misread the whole situation. He botched the whole mission by antagonising them. And instead of facing the conflict, he rewrote the history of the prophets: "A prophet is despised in his own country, among his own relations and in his own house." That was a very harsh and cruel thing to say, especially to those living in his own house. Do Jesus' parents despise him? I doubt it. More likely they can't understand what he's up to. Especially when, after saying what he did, he ups and goes, leaving them to live with the shame and the hurt of it all.

Innocent people suffer because Jesus never admits he has made a mistake. He exhorts the rest of us to be open and frank about our mistakes, to confess our sins, to acknowledge publicly our need of repentance. Fair enough, but he never gives leadership by example. Why open yourself up to someone who is as secret as the wilderness about his own mistakes and failings?

But Jesus' dishonesty does not stop there. Whatever turns out to be a flop is suddenly invested with eternal significance, as if it were meant to happen by decree. Even if Jesus got himself killed, I'm sure it would never be considered his own fault. Why is it that our failings are written up as wilful perversions whereas his are written off as providential opportunities? Who is kidding whom?

It would be easier to believe in Jesus if you thought he believed he was more like the rest of us.

He is different from us in many ways – his profuse talents put him in a league of his own – but not so different that he cannot tell us who or what is behind him. Throughout his teaching Jesus says: "You have heard it said to you...but I say to you..." When people then ask him the source of his authority, he refuses to answer. The questions are not impertinent: every teacher quotes his sources, but not Jesus. Why? Who formed him? Who taught him? Did he invent himself? Does he make it up as he goes along?

Although he leaks very little about himself, like all aspiring politicians he is anxious about his public reputation. His disciples can be heard polling the crowds about their opinions of Jesus: "What do you think of him? Who do you think he is?" Why does he wonder what we think of him when he never discloses who he is? What's the big secret? Is there a secret? Or is it that, after Nazareth, Jesus needs to create an aura of mystery about himself, to compensate for the poor polling returns in his home town? I don't know. Whatever the reason for the secrecy, it doesn't work. How can you trust a man who won't even tell you his name?

When it comes to naming the religious leaders, however, all coyness is gone. Jesus calls them arrogant, sadistic, sanctimonious, hypocritical, legalistic, blind fools. His vocabulary of abuse is extensive. He jokes about the way they dress in distinct religious garb, to stand out in a crowd, and caricatures their mannered ways with the vicious brilliance of a local comedian. For Jesus, religious leaders should be servants, nothing more; for him, therefore, those who lord it over others are merely pathetic icons of their pagan oppressors.

In spite of their manifest faults, our religious leaders are struggling with the difficult task of following the Law and keeping the people faithful to its observance. Jesus has no loyalty to the chief priests or the Pharisees or the scribes, but continues to rubbish them and disaffect their followers. Why doesn't he join one of the religious groups and reform it from within, instead of slinging mud from outside the ranks? Why does he dress up his bigotry as wisdom, when anyone with half a brain can see that he is envious of their earned authority over the people?

Jesus will want their downfall until it happens. He should be careful they don't return the compliment.

Although Jesus' accusations have some substance, none of our religious leaders could compete with him when it comes to conceit. Jesus' arrogance is matchless. He is always right, they are usually wrong; his ways lead to God's kingdom, their ways to blind alleys; he is the genuine article, they are all hypocrites. The comparisons are spurious. The world of religion, even to a shoemaker, is more nuanced and complex than that.

In debate Jesus has few equals, especially when it comes to warding off opponents. When cornered in any dispute he uses that neurotic defence tactic which attacks opponents while avoiding the issue. Take, for example, the recent incident in the Temple. The Pharisees and the scribes brought an adulterous woman to Jesus and asked him what he thought of the Mosaic ruling which condemned her to death by stoning. What does Jesus do? Answer them? Of course not! He focuses on their own track record in sinning, arousing their feelings of guilt and remorse. And they, the idiots, allow him to shift the ground of argument. Suddenly the accusers are the accused. Which of us is not guilty of sin? But that is not the issue, is it? Apart from that dishonesty, to make innocence a precondition for passing judgement would empty the synagogues and the Sanhedrin of religious leadership. But that's no problem to Jesus: that would serve his destructive purposes well.

In the Temple dispute the real issue for Jesus was to avoid conflict with the Roman authorities. He is a skilful politician. His tirades against our religious leaders are all the more puzzling in the light of his silence about our real oppressors. If Jesus wants to take on serious opposition, rather than hitting soft targets, why doesn't he address the brutal pagan presence that litters our promised land? When Jesus speaks about religion we can feel the clarifying force of an original mind; when he says nothing about Roman tyranny we can hear the expedient silence of a timid leader.

The Romans have nothing to fear from Jesus. With him their dominance is uncontested, their paganism is unmentioned, their brutality is ignored, the suffering they inflict on our people is unimportant.

I am no Zealot: I know that freedom does not

necessarily mean independence; I know that true liberty does not automatically arrive with native political power. Freedom is a burden, but surely it's better to be burdened with freedom than be resigned to slavery. Jesus can go on and on and on about freedom from Sabbath regulations, but not utter a whisper about freedom from despotic Rome.

Why does he avoid these major issues of justice, peace, freedom? Even Caiaphas, the leading Sadducee, risked confronting the Roman authorities when they tried to turn Jerusalem into a pagan shrine. And the high priest is regarded by many as a born-again collaborator.

Caiaphas would never dream of alienating our people by making a hero out of a Roman centurion. But Jesus did. To a man who earns his money oppressing Jews, Jesus says: "Never have I seen such faith in all of Israel." Never mind Abraham, Isaac, Jacob, Moses, David, Jeremiah. These are only dumb Jewish examples of faith! Who needs a Roman centurion as the hero of the Jewish faith? If that isn't genuflecting to your oppressor, what is? We need better heroes.

And what does Jesus have to say about Tiberius Caesar? "Give to Caesar what belongs to Caesar." Why should we render anything to Caesar? Caesar claims anything his legions can stamp their feet on. Caesar's appetite for real estate will only be satisfied when he owns the world. But perhaps it is little wonder Jesus refuses to oppose Caesar. Jesus says: "I have come to bring fire to the earth, and how I wish it were blazing already! Do you suppose I am here to bring peace on the earth? No, I tell you, but rather division. For from now on a household of five will be divided; three against two and two against three; the father divided against the son, son against father, mother against daughter, daughter against mother." Why this division? To fight against Caesar? No, rather for the sake of Jesus' kingdom. Caesar and Jesus are both alike: they will demolish all in front of them, no matter who the casualties are, to raise up their own prize kingdoms.

True to his own saying, among the first casualties in Jesus' kingdom were members of his own family. It was when I saw what happened to them that I decided it was time to give up running after Jesus and return home to my own family.

Jesus was invited to speak at the house of a rich patron. A crowd of us followed him, about fifty in number, and we were all welcomed graciously by the host. After the formalities, we sat in a circle around Jesus, in the atrium of the house. He started telling stories. I stayed at the back of the circle, near the door.

Soon after Jesus began, I became aware of a woman and two young men standing outside the open door. I wondered why they didn't come in. They looked rather anxious about something.

After some time the woman whispered to me in the softest of voices: "Sir, would you kindly give Jesus a message from me? Would you tell him that his mother and brothers are outside asking for him?"

I wondered why none of them could pass on the message, but I nodded to her.

I waited for a break in the storytelling, then stood up to get Jesus' attention. Everyone looked round. "Excuse me, Master," I said. "Your mother and brothers are standing outside asking for you."

Jesus looked up at me. "Who are my mother and brothers?" he asked. Then he looked around at those sitting in the circle about him and said: "Here are my mother and my brothers. Anyone who hears the word of

God and keeps it, that person is my mother and brother and sister."

I turned and looked back at the woman and the two young men. They were still standing outside. I was about to repeat the message, but it was obvious from their reaction they had heard. The three of them looked utterly bewildered, unsure what to do next.

I had an impulse to rush over to the woman and take her hand, I wanted desperately to say something that might ease her pain, tell her to hold fast to what she already had and not let go. But the moment of grace passed. Besides, who was I to give anyone advice?

I noticed her dig her fingernails into her palms and then, as if to hide the tears welling up in her eyes, she rearranged the veil that covered her head and shoulders. I could taste her pain. Every gesture she made seemed to happen in slow motion, as if she were relearning simple movements she once took for granted. I wondered if she was waiting for Jesus to come out to her.

By then the light was failing. The sky, I remember, looked drained of colour and life. The air was breathless. Behind me I could hear Jesus' voice, animated now as he led his hearers towards the climax of a story. I heard them all laugh in delight, and their laughter set off another story.

I heard one of the young men say to the woman: "Tomorrow perhaps. Tomorrow we can come back."

"Tomorrow..." she said and managed a smile.

I stood at the door, with my back to Jesus, watching the woman as she turned away, gathered herself, and faced the road for home. They walked away in silence, three people whose grief looked no less for being shared.

As I watched them go, I could not tell what it was, precisely, that reduced me to such despondency. Perhaps the feeling that, like Jesus, I had become an exile from my own family. Whatever it was, I took to the road and made for home.

Going home that day I felt like one of Jesus' characters, the runaway son who made his way home believing he had lost everything. But the one thing he had never lost was the love that was always there, still waiting for him, at home; a love that ran out to meet him, to make his journey shorter. My wife met me with a kindness and forgiveness that was embarrassing, and she then introduced me to the tiny bundle of flesh that is my beloved son.

I have settled back to work, making and mending shoes and sandals. Sometimes my wife asks me about my time away, and I try to respond to her as best I can. But more and more these days, her questions are about our future and family.

I tell her that I cannot imagine leaving home again, because I cannot imagine any messiah who would pull me away from them. They are real, they are mine, they are life, they are all I have. They make no large claims on me, just for my love and attention, and I give that with all my heart.

I think about Jesus often, especially in quiet moments when there is no one around and I am mending old worn shoes. I think of the brief time he was my hero, when everything seemed possible. I think of the time I hoped he would save us from oppression and sorrow and solitude. But that was not to be. So much hope, I keep telling myself, cannot be satisfied.

That "cannot be" gives me no delight, but grieves me more than I can say.

There is no ache more deadly than watching our hope

grow frail and infirm. We look on helplessly, knowing we can neither intervene nor walk away. We keep vigil. We light candles. We stumble around like sleepwalkers. Death comes. It happens so quickly, out of due season. And we feel cheated and impoverished and angry.

I mourn the loss of that hope. I am angry at Jesus for not turning out to be the person I hoped he would be; I am angry at myself for expecting him to go beyond our deceits but still be one of us; I am angry at God for allowing this useless pain to take its course. And there is a part of me, I admit, that feels scared of a future with no one like Jesus to believe in.

Perhaps I am just growing up. Perhaps. If growing up means taking the road of renunciation, learning to leave messiahs and kingdoms behind, relinquishing dreams, abandoning great expectations, moving on, accepting what is and what has to be, then my journey is well started.

More and more, it seems to me, life is about the art of sustaining losses. It's about embracing a disfigured world you know will never be healed. It's about living within the boundaries of the reachable and finding God locally. It's about recognising the simple truth that our battered lives can only be mended and repaired by attention and love.

That is no dreamy prospect. But it's the only one that will last.

NICODEMUS

Before seeking you out, I was troubled by a premonition that meeting you would be a serious mistake. Interesting, yes; but a mistake, all the same, because meeting you might make a claim on me, so it would be difficult to pretend afterwards that nothing much had happened. Now, as I lie here in the dead of night trying to get to sleep, that premonition seems to have proved its worth. At an hour when every good Jew is wrestling with his dreams, here am I wide awake staring at a darkness which seems to cover everything equally. I try not to take it in, but when I close my eyes I have no sense of being separate from the surrounding dark. It feels like being buried alive. At least I'm not dead, I think.

It has been like this every night since I met you. Like most people, I'd heard of your reputation as a healer and preacher, and how you were openly critical of religious authority. As a Pharisee myself I was hurt when I heard some of the things you were supposed to have said about us, but I'd been around long enough to know you might have a case. However, I couldn't be content with hearsay or a casual glimpse of you from the back of the crowd; besides, I was eager to see you privately, to take the measure of you, to form my own judgement about your worth. My curiosity, you see, was stronger than my apprehension.

I knew that at nightfall you retired to a small grove on the slopes of the Mount of Olives. It was there, on a moonless night, that I sought you out.

No one, of course, knew I was going to see you, not even you. Had I told my family or my colleagues, they would have thought I had taken leave of my senses, had grown into a daft old man who could astonish the Temple stones with his folly. As you know, I am a member of the Great Council; as you must know, I have a duty to protect the hierarchy's public image. It would be irresponsible for a highly placed ecclesiastic like myself to go openly to you: that could lead simple minds to think that the Sanhedrin was looking to you for leadership. And I doubt if Caiaphas, our president, would appreciate that – he who has always maintained that a politician is never off-duty, not even in his dreams.

So, I admit, the darkness suited me like an old cloak, giving me the cover and comfort I needed as I left here that night. The torch I carried stayed unlit.

The most difficult part was crossing the Kidron valley while avoiding the paths used by travellers and soldiers. Thankfully, I saw no one. For a short time I was followed by two mongrel dogs, but they soon lost interest in me and chased each other around the tombs, taking turns to play hunter and hunted. As I made my way up the slope of the Mount of Olives, I had to stop for breath. I felt tired and foolish and anxious; it was as if a dark angel had jostled me suddenly, warning me that I was out of my element and should turn back for home. At that moment I felt no longer innocent or ignorant.

I kept going, not knowing why. My whole body was heaving awkwardly, like a landed fish.

When I approached the grove I could see that your disciples were already asleep, lying stretched out around the fire. They had the look of sleeping sentries exhausted from the business of watching too long for some imaginary enemy. Their prostrate bodies, wrapped in cloaks against the cold, made curious shapes in the circle of faltering light. You were awake, a solitary vigilante, sitting on a stone, staring into the fire. When you heard my footsteps you looked up sharply and your whole body stiffened – like a gazelle alert to the presence of danger. I hesitated for a moment. I felt like running away, still unseen; instead, I stumbled, as if pushed, into the light where you could see me.

I tried to speak, but found myself only grinning stupidly. You were looking beyond me, as if expecting others to emerge from the dark. When none came, you motioned me to sit beside you.

When I sat down, your eyes were still hunting the dark behind me for some expected threat. Your restlessness bothered me, so reluctant were you to disregard any sound or movement beyond the range of the firelight. I could see sweat on your brow. None of this matched what I expected, and I didn't know how to react. A prize duo we made: a dumb ecclesiastic and a nervous prophet, waiting for what? It seemed neither right nor real. How I wished I was at home, in bed, in the dark, next to the assurance of my wife's warmth. And now that I am, I'm still back there with you in that grove.

It is strange, after years of standing upright in debates in Council, to find oneself bent and awkward in the presence of a prophet from Nazareth. There are some things in life nothing prepares you for, times when all those proven ways become so many useless voices.

After I introduced myself, I expressed my admiration for the signs you had worked, wonders that marked you as a man of God. You brushed aside my carefully rehearsed opening with a wave of your hand, as if admiration were the last thing needed.

"Why are you here, Nicodemus? What do you want me to do for you?"

Your questions, I must confess, took me by surprise. I gathered my knees up under my chin, as if that would help me to think. It was more difficult to gather my thoughts. I replied in general terms, saying how your preaching and works had made an impression on many people and that, because of this, I was keen to meet you myself. I began to sound like a celebrity addict. You didn't look impressed.

What you then said puzzled me. Only one thing mattered for those seeking God: a new start. You spoke of the kingdom of God and how no one could detect its presence or experience its power without being born again. New life needed new birth, you said, new possibility demanded new beginnings. To become a child of God, one had to be born again.

Do you remember my confusion? Any talk of change makes me feel insecure. I was already apprehensive about the future, and your insistence on new birth did nothing to calm my fears. We are born once, I said, and as soon as we leave the womb it closes behind us forever. Growing up means coming to terms with that original separation. Who can go back into the past, re-arrange experience, then re-emerge a new person? Even if it were possible, who would want to? We are stuck with our past. Our memory links us to the hopes we cherished and the losses we suffered, and these make us who we are. Who would recognise us if we were born again? Who would want us after so much change?

You must have thought I was either defensive or obtuse. New birth, you said, could happen at any time in life, since God was not fussed about the chronological age of his children. It was a new birth in the Spirit, not the flesh; it did not change where we came from or how we arrived at the present, only the way we were going. Think on that, you said, think on it.

I nodded, hoping you would think I had understood everything you had said. You stood up. I thought you were bringing our meeting to a close, but you had risen to rekindle the fire that had been left to burn itself out while everyone slept. I was keeping you awake. I wondered if I should go. You knelt down beside the ashes, sifting them until you uncovered a few embers; then coaxing the smouldering remains into a flicker of life, you slowly built up the fire with the tinder that had been collected for next morning. One or two of the sticks seemed to catch fire, but expired as quickly, leaving everything dark again; then a tiny flame asserted itself and gradually fired some of the other sticks until they crackled and flamed. You waited on your knees beside the fire, like some persistent doctor waiting for a patient to respond, until the flames were large enough to cope with the piece of wood you wanted to put on top. That done, you rose from your knees, turned to me and smiled, and came across to sit on the ground beside me.

Neither of us spoke. We watched and waited to see if the last piece of wood would take.

If any night travellers had passed on the upper road and spotted the two of us, they might have mistaken us for two insomniacs whose shared affliction had excluded us from the circle of sleepers. Your disciples slept on; one of them, disturbed by the light of the new fire, pulled his cloak nearer his face and turned over to face the comfort of darkness.

The wind, I remember, was blowing the smoke away

from us and carrying it off in the direction of the Kidron valley. As I watched the traces disappear I heard a voice that seemed to come from a far distance, from way across the valley:

"Nicodemus, you must be born again."

The voice, of course, was yours. Its personal note, to be honest, made me a little angry, a little defiant. Me? Born again?

I'm too long in the tooth to start again. As an old boy from an old school I am securely rooted in the old certainties that our ancestors have formed over two centuries. I'm not one of God's fanatics, like John the Baptist was, but I am faithful to the Law and I have come to love God more than anyone I have ever loved. Surely that has to be enough. How can I do more?

I am too old to masquerade as an innocent, a child of some new dawning, a fresh arrival in your kingdom. To assume I could do that would be perverse, an evasion of everything I am. I don't want to end my days in this unmendable world playing the part of an old pretender. The world around me doesn't impress me enormously, but it's the place where I live and move and manage. I am part of its fragility and see no point in turning my back on it. I am alive with all that is behind me, so I have no yearning to shrug off the old man and be born again. For what? For a change?

I am no great believer in change. So often change ends up merely making a commotion, devising a ritual of thrill that leaves you empty when the applause has died down and everyone has gone home to continue real life. I have lost the appetite, if ever I had it, for new horizons, new hopes, new deals. When I hear talk of these I can never silence older echoes in my head. We still have to honour the vision we are committed to as God's chosen people.

We have to catch up with our past. We are a history of great yesterdays.

I prefer to be an old man kneeling in the graveyard of my ancestors and pledging myself anew to their dreams than a new recruit in your kingdom. Forgive me for saying this, but your kingdom is too unearthed for those of us who grew up to trust our religion and its practical landmarks.

We don't need change or new commandments or new leaders. What we need is reverence for our tradition, loyalty to its laws, obedience to those God in his wisdom has appointed to rule us.

I know you criticise our leaders – I am one of them – and much of what you say is true. But tell me this: if God himself appointed archangels over us, do you think it would be any different? I no longer cherish the illusion that any messiah will save us from ourselves, that any leader can bear the weight of our enterprises and hopes. If we make our leaders into gods, we should cease wondering why they fail us so quickly. No, we're not dying from lack of leadership or enlightenment; we're dying from lack of personal purpose in our lives.

I must have offended you. So much argument just to stay put and defend the status quo. The ramblings of an old loyalist. But if tradition means holding on to what we love, what else could I do?

"If you believe everything you have said, Nicodemus, why are you here? It isn't satisfaction that has brought you out here in the middle of the night."

That question again. I admitted I wasn't wholly content with my life. But who is? Like everyone else I have a sense of incompleteness about who I am and where I am going. But that is hardly a major affliction, more a minor chronic ailment that comes with being human.

Dissatisfaction gives you a reason for getting up in the morning, it motivates you to keep going.

I am not claiming I have no need to change anything in my life. Sure, I have to make changes. Nothing huge, though. Anyway, how can all this change come about? That was my question then, and that is my question now as I lie here swaddled in darkness, leaking grudges into my pillow.

Remember how you insisted that I, a teacher of Israel, should know these things? "Look around you. The wind blows wherever it pleases; you can hear its sound, but you cannot tell where it comes from or where it is going. Who knows the wind? Who knows the Spirit of God? Like the wind, the Spirit is only known by the effect it produces in life. And the effect is always change, change for the better."

To compare the working of the Spirit to the drifting of the wind is to make a subversive parallel, one that could signal the destruction of institutional religion. We have learned that God has revealed himself primarily through the Law. This truth protects us from becoming unmoored from tradition, drifting towards a storm of charismatic voices all claiming to speak for God. Certainly, God spoke through the prophets, but they were the guardians of memory who called people back to the established covenant. Our God is unchanging. The wind is fickle shifting, unpredictable. It submits to no control and recognises no boundary. How can the Spirit of God move like that? How could belief in that kind of God be reconciled with our identity as the people of God and our religion of convention?

How can I, a teacher of Israel and a spokesman for its tradition, learn anything from the wind?

It was disturbing to have you challenge our religious

security as if it were a fiction devised to distract us from the consequences of God's freedom. The rest of us don't share your awesome independence, your reluctance to attach yourself to any one person or place, your compulsion to disturb the fragile peace that so many good people are committed to preserve.

If disturbing the peace is a crime in every society, then you are verging on the criminal. I am afraid for you. Already the Great Council seems intent on convicting you, and when I protested in the assembly that our Law gives you the right to a hearing, they asked me: "Are you a Galilean?" I knew what they were saying, but I said to myself: whatever you say, say nothing. Then they warned me: "Prophets do not come from Galilee."

Their confidence disturbs me more than your questions. And I'm sure it's only a matter of time before you become a victim of their criminal certainty.

Curiously, some of the Council suspect that I am one of your confidential agents. Since the recent assembly I've been wondering if they got wind of my night visit to you. If they do find out, I'm finished. They will find a replacement for me. That worries me. I must be careful.

What surprises me is that no one has asked me outright if I have met you personally. That question will come. What can I say? Deny it? No, I don't think so. Admit it, but confess to a lapse of judgement? Perhaps. Tell them that talking to you was a most disconcerting experience? That would be true. I don't know what to think, never mind what to say. But it's only a matter of time before I am forced to say something.

Perhaps I should tell the assembly how our meeting ended that night, how our strange encounter came to a close. Do you remember? I do. I remember it as if it were still happening.

The night had turned colder. I remember feeling a stiffness in my back and neck, an old complaint, and I started moving my shoulders up and down. The fire looked as if it was closing down, and in the diminished light it was difficult to make out much of anything. I began to think of home, of getting back, of slipping quietly into the warmth of my bed without disturbing my wife. Lingering in your cold hide-out, I was sure, could serve no useful purpose to either of us.

When I looked across at you, I could see the upper part of your body slumped forward. You were holding your head in your hands as if it were a large wound. At that moment you didn't look as if you could be a threat to anyone.

I felt sorry for you, for all the shabby returns you must get for your efforts, for the times your hope is wasted on the likes of me. Were you wondering why I resisted you, why my change would not happen, why I was absenting myself from your programme of renewal? Or were you just exhausted from a tiring day that had run into a wearisome night?

As if you guessed my concern, you lifted your head and turned to look at me. When you spoke, your voice was low and intense, almost pleading:

"Tell me something before you go, Nicodemus. What do you think? Once there was a father who had two sons, both of whom he loved with a full heart. He went and said to the first, 'My son, you go and work in the vineyard today.' The son had other plans, friends to meet, places to go. He refused bluntly: 'I will not go.' Afterwards he regretted his refusal and went to the vineyard. The father made the same request of the other son. This son had other plans, friends to meet, promises to keep. He agreed readily: 'Certainly, sir.' But he didn't turn up at the vineyard that day. Which of the two sons did the father's will?"

"The first," I said.

You nodded, then looked away.

I was unsure if I was expected to say more, but I had nothing more to say. I waited. Nothing. The only thing I could hear was the murmur of the wind.

I rose, stretched, and pulled my cloak closer around me. It was time to go. I picked up my torch from the ground and moved over to the fire. In the midst of the ashes a few embers were still glowing. I stirred the remains of the fire and waited for the torch to catch and flame. The sudden light felt strange, like an intruder.

Behind me, I could hear you getting up. I turned towards you. Without looking at your face, I crossed over to you, took your right hand, bent over and kissed it.

"Goodnight, Nicodemus. God go with you."

"Master, goodnight. God stay with you."

I turned away, leaving you in the dark behind me. And I retraced my steps for home.

CAIAPHAS

When I married the daughter of Annas the high priest, I suspected that my career prospects would be dramatically improved. The priestly aristocracy in Jerusalem is a small world – most of the thousands of priests and levites wandering around the city are oafs in fancy dress – and during the nine years Annas exercised the office of high priest, he used his considerable influence to establish a family dynasty among the chief priests. By the time he was deposed by the Roman procurator Valerius Gratus, the ruling house of Annas was securely established and I was married into the family.

The next three years saw a rapid succession of three high priests, all relatives of Annas. They arrived and disappeared so quickly that ordinary people had little time to remember their names. All three were noted in the Sanhedrin for their cleverness and self-confidence; but, like all clever people, they became bored easily and grew careless in their disappointment. They overslept too much. If their cleverness was not enough to defeat them, their inflated self-confidence sealed their fate, for it dulled whatever talent they had for survival. They forgot one simple truth: high priests are always on approval. Always.

When my appointment as high priest arrived from

Rome, it came as no surprise to my father-in-law, or to me, that I was to follow in his footsteps.

Now, twelve years on, people joke that I have become something of a fixture as high priest. I know I am no fixture. But one thing is certain: people know how to spell my name.

From the very beginning my policy has been to maintain good relations with the Roman occupying power without prejudicing either the security of our ruling house or the integrity of our Jewish religion. This has not been easy. My survival depends on Rome's approval, but Rome knows that for me to be an effective public servant, I must earn the critical approval of my own people. As a colonising power, the Romans will never appoint a Zealot to the office of high priest; but neither do they want to install an echo chamber, a ventriloquist's dummy that could never command the respect of our people. Rome looks to someone who, given the political circumstances, has developed a sense for what is possible and what will be tolerated. An intellectual pragmatist.

Playing the role requires agility and courage. Let me give an example. When Pontius Pilate arrived in Caesarea to take up his new appointment as procurator, he was shocked to learn there was no statue of Caesar in Jerusalem. Granted, this monumental absence is unusual, since in every city square throughout the Roman empire there is a statue of the emperor, before which passers-by have to bow. But this abominable practice is against the first and second commandments of the Decalogue. If the new procurator was aware of this, it made no impression on him: he was determined to bring Jerusalem into line with other Roman cities.

The first time Pilate arrived in Jerusalem, the soldiers of his entourage were ordered to carry images of the emperor on their standards. Pilate's entry into Jerusalem was a procession of provocation and insult. When the soldiers reached the Antonia Fortress, they placed the graven images on the walls overlooking the Temple. After this was done, Pilate returned to Caesarea, where he waited for us to attack the fortress. Clearly, he wanted a Jewish revolt to enliven the beginning of his term of office.

The whole of Jerusalem looked to me for leadership. What was I going to do? This outrage could not be allowed to pass, but neither could we afford to attack the fortress – that would have been mass suicide. I sent a high-ranking delegation of chief priests to Pilate's immediate superior, the Roman governor of Syria, reminding him that Caesar Augustus had promised Jerusalem immunity from the imperial cult. That done, I organised a protest march to Caesarea.

About eight thousand of us marched to the sea and camped outside Pilate's residence. For a whole week we picketed the palace. We chanted prayers for the conversion of the procurator. Loudly. Every time Pilate emerged, the volume increased. His wife stayed indoors.

Throughout the days and nights a continuous wail was to be heard in Caesarea. For the ships sailing into harbour, the mournful cries must have sounded like ten thousand Rachels refusing to be consoled. Strangers must have wondered what massacre had taken place, or what desolation was about to happen, to bring forth such a keening of spirits.

Something had to give. Pilate had to do something. We, for our part, would not compromise.

Pilate responded. He gave his commanders the order for the troops to surround us. The cavalry then pressed us tighter together until we were all crushed into a mass huddle; the foot soldiers behind them, armed with long shields, banged anyone attempting to escape, back into the mass of flesh. At Pilate's signal, the soldiers drew their swords. We all went quiet, as if struck dumb. Pilate waited. We all waited.

If Pilate was hoping that our fear of holocaust would make us submit to what our hearts and minds could never tolerate, he was to learn the stamina of the people he was appointed to govern.

From somewhere in the middle of all our crushed bodies a voice started to chant Kaddish, the prayers for the dead. We all picked up the familiar notes, believing we were chanting the dirge for ourselves.

Pilate's nerve broke. From where I was I could see the sweat of recognition on his brow. He spoke to his commanders and turned away. Orders were shouted; swords were sheathed; the soldiers withdrew, deprived of their exercise. I was given the message that the graven images would be dismantled. Before we began our journey back, I told the crowds that we would journey quietly. There would be no victory chants, no triumphant procession, no vulgar displays of religious superiority. They obeyed.

By the time we reached Jerusalem, the walls of the Antonia Fortress were clear again.

Speaking frankly, it is an exhausting business trying to accommodate a foreign power and protect one's religious and cultural traditions. The love of religious freedom is more easily come by than the will to ensure it, which is why we Sadducees devote ourselves to the delicate task of leading our people carefully and cautiously. Sometimes we have to be assertive, otherwise our people would lose their very identity; other times we have to compromise with the Romans in the give and take of our imperfect situation.

Curiously, our main opponents are not the Roman officials but the Pharisees. They hate compromise. They communicate by dogma and decree with all the certainty of inhibited religious, and they enjoy an influence over the common people that is unwarranted by their real status in life. Some of the Pharisees are good men, beyond reproach; most of them, however, are possessed with the excessive commitment and intolerance of the true fanatic.

As religious teachers, the Pharisees are forever striving after impossible goals, as if the unrealisable is what is significant. They believe in the perfectibility of people, and their curriculum of progress is crowded with tedious details covering every eventuality. We Sadducees accept only the written Law; the Pharisees hedge the Law around with a maze of rules, customs and traditions that would confuse almighty God.

Their unremitting ethic of self-improvement makes them neurotic and mischievous: privately, they are fascinated by their own spiritual health; publicly, they are obsessed with the failings of others. Living as they do in a world of anxious comparisons, they often appear edgy, humourless, unforgiving. Much of their time seems devoted to catching people out – like so many spiders spinning webs to entrap passing innocents.

Out of their compulsion for perfection, they manufacture a curious theology: that God is keenly interested in the details of the human story, monitoring every moment of every life in every age. Their religious influence is so powerful among the people that this belief has grown into an epidemic delusion. Personally, I find it blasphemous: it makes the all holy God out to be indistinguishable from the nosy village widow whose energy is consumed by the need to know everyone's business.

The Pharisees load God with history and the particularity that crowds it. They should learn from their own scripture what Job learned from life: that God is far beyond our petty lives and decisions, because he is above all evil. We have only to consult our experience to know that God has left us, for better or worse, to get on with the business of living. It is we ourselves who control our destiny. To believe otherwise is to deny the teaching of experience.

Unlike the Pharisees, we Sadducees do not believe in the recent doctrine of the resurrection or the endurance of the soul.

We are traditionalists; the Pharisees are new conservatives. We promise no heaven of reward, we threaten no hell of punishment: the best and the worst we ever get is where we are. And if our only promised land is here, our only time to enjoy its fruits is now.

It was a group of Pharisees from Galilee who first brought to my notice the existence of Jesus of Nazareth. They reported that Jesus had openly criticised them for their bleak religious outlook, for inventing new burdens for an already overburdened people, and for refusing to lift a finger to help them. This information did not displease me. As far as I was concerned, the criticism was well deserved and might serve to temper the common people's reverence towards the Pharisees. Were this to happen, I thought, this Jesus of Nazareth would be my secret ally.

On the other hand, I was concerned. I had little sympathy for the Pharisees, but what if Jesus did not stop at criticising them? As the poet Horace noted: "For it is your business, when the wall next door catches fire."

When I heard that Jesus had gathered his own followers and was attracting crowds as he made his way south to Jerusalem, I appointed agents to monitor events and report back to me personally. Good intelligence is never wasted.

One night, soon after this, I was voicing my concern to my wife. Dinner was over, the guests had gone away satisfied, and we were sitting quietly enjoying the peace that follows a good reception. As I talked, I watched her fingers move surely and elegantly as she embroidered the hem of a new liturgical robe.

"Anyway, this Jesus can hardly be a threat to the likes of us," I said. "He is only a Galilean, a carpenter from the outback. But it's prudent to take precautions. From where I sit, you can never be too careful."

My wife dropped her needle.

Jesus' name kept appearing with disturbing regularity in my agents' reports. Their independent accounts converged on several points. Jesus was a popular preacher and healer; he was not attached to any known religious group, but retained a critical independence; his select followers were mostly Galilean fishermen; he frequently challenged the rules for interpreting Sabbath obligations; his message concentrated on the kingdom of God; he regularly shared his table with known sinners; he was openly critical of religious authority. By all accounts, his popularity was due to his wonder-working, which attracted the masses desperate to decorate their boring lives with ornaments of wonder.

What emerged from these reports disturbed me: because of what Jesus did and said, claims were being made about who he really was. His impact on people was so marked that they were beginning to think he was the messiah. The

Galileans had gone further by trying to make him their king, a political act that could only have grave results.

A messianic pretender was all that was needed to destroy the working relationship with the Roman authorities that had taken me years to build. If Roman intelligence discovered that the Jewish leadership was consenting by silence to a Galilean claim to kingship, our whole nation would be in jeopardy. It was time for me to act.

As president of the governing body of the Jewish nation I called together the seventy-one members of the Sanhedrin, to discuss the Jesus affair. I was sure of the support of the chief priests and most of the elders; the scribes, however, many of whom were Pharisees, were another question. When I outlined the danger that Jesus posed to the internal stability of our nation and our relations with the Roman authorities, and that the political and religious aspects of this case were inseparable, many members did not seem to grasp the situation at all. (It has never ceased to surprise me how many religious people believe that political obtuseness is akin to virtue.)

The Sanhedrin was divided about what to do about Jesus. Some liberal Pharisees were well disposed to the Galilean, even though they had serious reservations about his teaching. Some orthodox Pharisees, for whom the Law remained the sole means of relating to God, were anxious that I would use my authority to denounce Jesus as a false teacher, one who consistently refused to recognise legitimate religious authority. They quoted Deuteronomy: "If anyone presumes to disobey either the priest who is there in the service of God, or the judge, that man must die. You must banish this evil from Israel. And all the people shall hear of it and be afraid and not act presumptuously a second time." They reminded me of my obligation to pronounce on Jewish orthodoxy. One of them summed up the argument: "Anyone who defies your authority in the exercise of your judicial function must by our Law be put to death. About this there can be no doubt or debate."

The proposal was made: Jesus of Nazareth, false prophet and messianic pretender, should be put to death.

When this was voiced, Nicodemus signalled his desire to speak. He looked his usual anxious self, as if he alone in the world was tormented by the complexities of the issue before us. A liberal Pharisee, too impressionable to be trusted, Nicodemus is known as a man whose life is crippled by caution and indecision. He wants to please people, he desperately wants to be liked. When I recognised him, he stood up. My heart sank. Like many others, I was afraid we were going to be treated to another of his tortuous, agonising speeches. He is the kind of man who will lecture people from sunrise to sunset on a variety of issues; but it would be easier to get a man to rise from the dead than to get Nicodemus to commit himself publicly to an issue. When pressed, he always wants more time to consider, more information to hand, stubborn in making a virtue out of not knowing what to think. And when it comes to the time of resolution, he is indefatigable in indecision. Were he an army commander, you would always feel secure on the other side.

Nicodemus had waited until the murmuring had died down and he had everyone's undivided attention. He did not speak immediately, of course. He had to have time to be seen to gather his thoughts; we had to have time to recognise the philosopher's burden weighing on him.

Annas leaned over to me and whispered: "That man has the patience of the true egoist. He should be in the theatre, not the Sanhedrin."

After clearing his throat, Nicodemus said: "Surely the Law does not allow us to pass judgement on a man without first giving him a hearing and learning what he does."

I was amused by this intervention – Nicodemus playing the role of the fair-minded innocent, when I knew from my reports that he had sought Jesus out on the Mount of Olives. Poor old Nicodemus, I thought, always trying to postpone difficult decisions, always trying to project himself as the spokesman for reasonableness. His crafted innocence was becoming something of a bore.

I said nothing.

One of the chief priests asked him: "Are you from Galilee too? Search the scriptures, if you have the patience, and you will see that no prophet, never mind a messiah, is to rise from Galilee."

Everyone waited for Nicodemus to reply, but he would need a week to think about it. He may have had the brains to argue a defence of Jesus, but he was certainly not equipped with the guts. He looked vaguely about him, as if some other voice might support him. When none did, he sat down. We were to be spared a harangue.

I knew that the differences were so great among the factions in the Sanhedrin that no agreement could be reached at that sitting. Although there was general agreement that Jesus was unorthodox and a threat to public order, there was no consensus on what to do about him. There was little point in continuing the debate. I reminded the members that although we were allowed to deal with religious offences and internal civic affairs in our courts, we did not enjoy *ius gladii,* the right of passing a capital sentence. Only the Roman procurator had that authority. Concluding the meeting, I promised the Sanhedrin that Jesus would be monitored closely, thanked them for their attention, and told them we might be pressed to make some decision in the near future.

Clearly, I had to think again.

Events could not have worked out better if I had organised them myself. The way Jesus chose to enter Jerusalem was an act of political suicide. From Bethphage he led a rag-bag parade of supporters down the Mount of Olives, up past the Antonia Fortress, through the city gates, across open markets, along the narrow, curving streets to the Temple precincts. He was sitting on a donkey, looking ill at ease as crowds of visiting pilgrims half-heartedly cheered him, without knowing what they were cheering.

This was my first sight of Jesus: he looked more victim than victor. Many of the Galilean pilgrims joined the followers of Jesus in screaming treason: "Blessed is he who comes as king!" I watched this carnival of impertinence from a distance: it was sheer gift. I looked to see if Nicodemus was among those following Jesus, but he was nowhere to be seen. If he was watching this, what further evidence would he need?

Jesus dismounted and entered the Temple precincts. In the outer court, open to Gentiles as well as Jews, business is conducted necessary for the maintenance of cult, so that animals which meet the ritual requirements are available for worshippers to offer sacrifice. There are thousands of animals: oxen, sheep, goats, pigeons; also for sale is incense, wine, salt, and oil. None of these can be purchased with coins carrying pagan symbols, so money-changers perform the essential service of changing foreign and unacceptable currency into local coinage.

As if demented, Jesus started charging around the Court of the Gentiles, screaming at traders, overturning tables, releasing doves, whacking oxen, kicking jars.

Some chief priests and scribes tried to calm him down, but he became hysterical as he accused them of turning the Temple into a shopping precinct. When I saw the Temple police move in to arrest Jesus, I signalled to the captain to leave Jesus untouched. This uncontrolled display of contempt would serve our purposes well.

I could see how the Galileans were enjoying the chaos: the northern theatre of revolt had come to play in the southern sanctuary of tradition. When their hero had calmed down, he began to preach in the Temple as if the place were his rightful preserve. At the heart of his message was the blasphemous claim against the heart of our religion: he would destroy the Temple, for its time had come. No, my friend, I said to myself: in a world of uncertainties I will ensure one thing is certain: it will be the Temple that will destroy you, for sure.

It was time to move in for the kill.

Two days after the Temple incident, a small group of chief priests and the captain of the Temple police came to see me. The chief priests reported a strange visit from one of Jesus' close followers, Judas Iscariot by name, who warned them that Jesus was organising a Galilean uprising, set for the festival of Passover.

"Do you trust this Judas?" I asked.

"How can you completely trust a traitor?" one of them replied.

"Did he ask for money?"

"No."

"Did you reward him with any?"

"No."

"Then how does he benefit by telling us this?"

"Protection. He is scared of being executed as one of Jesus' followers."

"If that is so, why doesn't he take this information to the Romans?"

"He despises the Romans. He believes this is a matter for the Jewish authorities, since Jesus claims to be the messiah."

"Is he coming back to see you?"

"Yes. He said he would keep us informed."

"Test the sincerity of this Judas," I said. "We have already decided to arrest Jesus the night after next. We already know where he stays, in Gethsemane, on the Mount of Olives. Tell Judas we will believe him if he leads the Temple police to Jesus. If he agrees, pay him. If he refuses to co-operate, keep him in custody. But arrest Jesus, anyway, and bring him to my palace."

They agreed, then took their leave.

It was up to me to inform the Sanhedrin. It was up to me to arrange an ending.

The arrest took place last night, according to plan, and Jesus was brought to my palace for interrogation. A small representative group of chief priests, elders and scribes sat with me. The purpose of the night hearing was to rehearse the charges and discover the defence, to expedite proceedings when the Supreme Council met this morning. In case Jesus contested any of the charges last night, I had a number of witnesses on stand-by, agents who had listened to his teachings and noted deviances from the Law. But, as it turned out, I did not need them.

Throughout the interrogation Jesus refused to answer a single question I put to him, electing to play the silent captive. When I listed the serious charges against him, he answered not a word. He ignored my appeals to speak in his own defence or nominate his own witnesses. I even invited him to call in his assistant Simon Peter who, I was informed, was standing outside, warming himself in the courtyard. I thought the presence of his closest associate might at least be a comfort. I waited for the reply. Silence. All I could hear was a cock crowing in the dark.

The hearing was proving a waste of time; I was beginning to feel slightly foolish; the other councillors were becoming impatient. It seemed, as indeed one of my agents had reported, that Jesus was too whole-hearted about his mission in life to avoid its consequences. His silence was an admission of his inability to compromise. The more I looked at him, the more I realised how dangerous and arrogant a leader he would make if we allowed him his freedom.

I ordered the guards to throw him into the dungeon. The hearing that turned out to be no hearing was concluded.

There was no point in bringing Jesus before the full session of the Sanhedrin when it met this morning. I explained to the council that the prisoner had refused to recognise my authority, but that his silent contempt did not absolve us from the responsibility of passing judgement. In fact his contempt for my authority as high priest was ground enough for condemnation, a point mentioned at our previous meeting.

I knew, of course, that proceeding with this argument would be risky, even after the recent happenings. Some influential voices might still argue there were insufficient grounds for condemning Jesus. Claiming to be king of the Jews is not a capital charge in our Law. But for an individual to claim kingship in Roman occupied territory is high treason. In my final speech, therefore, I shifted the ground of the argument.

"It is not our task to interfere unreasonably with others, to ridicule their beliefs, to question their lawful pursuits. We are religious leaders, not miniature Caesars. But neither can we, by default, allow this Galilean agitator to flout our conventions and ignore our authority, allow him to be proclaimed king of the Jews, allow him and his partisans free passage through the streets of our capital city, allow him to take over the Temple and then vow to destroy it, allow him to act as a focus of opposition to religious and civil authority.

"I say we cannot sanction any of this. But, honourable members, we have already sanctioned all of it. This I say with shame on my face.

"We have been silent. But we fool ourselves if we believe that our silence has enhanced our moral authority. On the Jesus affair this high council has voiced no public protest, formed no judgement, passed no ruling. When Jesus has invited the populace again and again, 'Come to me all you who labour and are overburdened and I will give rest', again and again we have stood by idly, watching our people leave us and go to him for help. Our silence and our idleness have been interpreted not as a neutral act but as religious permission, even political impotence. Our silence has helped Jesus as if we had equipped him with weapons for his cause.

"When we equip a rival we sacrifice something of our own authority and independence. Gentlemen, we have sacrificed enough; we have been silent for too long; we can fuss and dither no more. Our silence convicts us as accomplices in the prisoner's claim to be king of the Jews.

"Answer me this, if you will. Do you think the Romans were all asleep when Jesus' messianic parade passed the walls of the Antonia Fortress? Do you think that Pilate has no informers on the streets of Jerusalem? Do you think the Romans will stand by idle if we continue to permit a fellow Jew to claim kingship and permit his followers to so acknowledge him?

"We are all in danger. We could all be cancelled tomorrow. You know as well as I do that to proclaim someone as the messiah is an act of political subversion, for it is to assert the end of Roman rule. The Romans are not unaware of the implications of our theology.

"In this council Jesus has his apologists as well as his critics, a difference that reflects the wide range of views we hold on many issues. But I am unaware of anyone who believes him to be the messiah. I may be mistaken. I am open to correction. If any of you believe that Jesus of Nazareth is the messiah, you should declare that belief in the midst of this assembly. Now."

At this point in my speech I waited. I looked around at the faces I know so well. I waited to see if any hands were raised, if anyone was rising to speak. I looked over at Nicodemus, but he was staring at the floor, lost in his own world of thought.

"Will anyone defend Jesus' claim to kingship?" I asked.

Nobody moved. Nobody said anything.

I continued. "If you do not believe this claim, it follows that you must believe Jesus to be an impostor. Thus believing, you have an obligation to protect the integrity of our religion and our nation's safekeeping by condemning the prisoner.

"We are not debating the fate of an individual prisoner. We are debating the fate of our people, the fate of the Temple, the fate of our religious freedom under Roman rule. For the sake of all that we hold dear, we have to reject Jesus and his claims.

"I am sympathetic to the point that many of you have made, that Jesus' popularity with the people might make it difficult for us to survive as the architects of his death. But this problem is answered by my proposal.

"Our powers are inadequate to deal with Jesus. I am asking you, therefore, to vote that our prisoner be handed over to the Roman authorities, on the capital charge of treason. The Romans can then shoulder the responsibility for the death of Jesus, while this assembly's diplomatic standing with Rome will not be in question.

"In voting yes to my proposal you will be voting for the safekeeping of our people. Our urge to protect them and our condemnation of Jesus merge into one issue. It is only right that one man should die for the sake of the people. Anyone who opposes Jesus' condemnation is putting our people at risk and our freedom in jeopardy. And that would be treason of the most terrible kind.

"I ask you now to vote: that Jesus of Nazareth be handed over to the Roman procurator, on the capital charge of high treason."

I sat down. I started praying for a clean finish to this whole messy business.

The vote was taken. The result was unanimous. There were no abstentions.

One hour ago I handed the prisoner over to the authority of Pontius Pilate. I shall let that displaced horse-dealer play his part in the drama. For the rest, we can all sleep more easily in our beds.

PONTIUS PILATE

I have always regarded myself as a reasonable man and a conscientious public servant, something of an example to those who work in the field of foreign affairs. Dutiful to a fault, my wife says. Pompous Pilate, my detractors say. From the time I donned my *toga virilis* I have enjoyed the best in diplomatic training, and my skills in artful management, supported by a robust use of force, have been tested and refined in a number of outposts throughout the Roman Empire. As a reward for my labours I expected something more prestigious than being fifth governor of this backwater. Judaea is not a coveted post in diplomatic circles, not a place to make a name for yourself, not even a civilized hideout. It is a home for displaced fanatics, a circus for religious exhibitionists. Believe me, I preside over a madhouse.

No matter how hard one works here, the common people remain stubbornly blind to the benefits of the Pax Romana. For them, the Pax Romana is no more than the eagle's dominance over its chosen territory. But what do these people know? They are backward, boorish, perverse, superstitious, priest-ridden. Their religion makes them very foreign foreigners. Wherever you have people fascinated by religion, you get a lot of borderline cases. Most of their priests who strut around Jerusalem are honourable members of the lunatic fringe, and under all his purple dye Caiaphas is certifiably homicidal.

When I first came here, I believed it would be difficult to govern a people united by a dangerous memory, a history of shared suffering; but I soon discovered so many factions among them – religious, political, tribal, cultural, geographical – that I have come to believe only the Roman presence can contain their mad rivalries.

If there is no hatred to compete with family hatred, no bitterness to match the kind reserved for kinsfolk, then Jerusalem is the world centre of family squabbling.

Rivalry is written in their stars: you only have to read their scripture to see that for yourself. No sooner does the first family become established than fratricide becomes fashionable and doing business with God becomes a deadly affair. If life made Cain and Abel into a farmer and a shepherd, religion made them into an executioner and a victim. We are told that Cain brought the produce of the soil as an offering to God, while his brother Abel brought the first-born of the flock. The God of Israel showed an early preference for younger brothers, shepherds, and slaughtered lamb. And instead of quarrelling with God, the real villain of the drama, Cain dragged his brother into the killing fields and relieved him of his life. Why? Perhaps Cain thought that the blood of his brother would be more acceptable to his tyrannical God than the blood of the lamb. Who knows?

(All right, I hear you say, but Rome's beginnings had its own prize duo, what with Romulus slaying Remus for laughing at the walls he built surrounding the Palatine. Yes, my friend, but the obnoxious Remus provoked his twin brother, whereas Abel was an innocent who became an offering. Romulus suffered public humiliation; Cain suffered only liturgical disappointment. Hardly a reason for a just war.)

If Cain, patron saint of the disaffected, was condemned to be a wanderer and fugitive, one thing is for sure: all his bruised descendants have ended up pitching their tents in this godforsaken place.

Do not misunderstand me: I am not arguing against hostility in itself. That would be foolish. The whole of nature thrives on conflict, just as the whole of political life thrives on opposition. Without hostility, things fall apart. We all need our enemies to sharpen our identity and define our standards. But the crowd of barbarians I govern don't need the Romans for hostility; they manage very well by themselves.

So why, you may ask, did I agree to come here? For the same reasons, I suppose, that most of us in the foreign service say yes to disagreeable postings. Because the occupational habit of obedience to superiors inevitably means habitual suppression and compromise. Because our own career hopes begin to dull without the sanction of public appointment and approval. Because dissembling is the way we institutional men manage to survive. More to the point, perhaps, because it is better to govern Cain's descendants than be third secretary in a spa resort for Roman matrons.

Some of my friends tell me that I am lucky to be alive. They warn me to do nothing that might give Rome reasons to doubt my loyalty. Let me explain. Although I was appointed by Tiberius, my patron was Lucius Aelius Sejanus, then prefect of the praetorian guard and favourite of the emperor. Sejanus was a man whose influence was matched by his ambition: his real goal was to be nominated by Tiberius as his heir designate. Sejanus had Tiberius' only son, Drusus, poisoned. He then encouraged the shy and distrustful emperor to withdraw from the vexations of public life and retire to Capreae. With Tiberius out of the way, Sejanus was in sole possession of power. He cleared the field of possible rivals. Two years ago Tiberius woke up to what was happening, wrote from Capreae to the senate and commanded the execution of Sejanus, his family and supporters.

You understand why I have to be careful.

At the moment, Jerusalem is overflowing with pilgrims arriving for the feast of Passover. That is the official description. What is really happening is that caravans of religious louts come up to Jerusalem for their annual blood sports, hoping for trouble with the authorities. There is usually more than slaughtered lamb on the festival menu. That is why I am here. My official residence is at the port of Caesarea, on the coast of the Great Sea, which serves as a military base for most of the three thousand mercenaries under my command. There is a cohort stationed here in Jerusalem; all the same, I always bring a good number of my garrison here for the Passover, to ensure that the troops can stay on full alert.

While in Jerusalem we stay here at the Antonia Fortress, which adjoins the north wall of the Temple precincts. Although the Temple overlooks the city, the Antonia dominates the Temple. In this violent city even the architecture thrives on hostility.

Claudia my wife has come with me this time. She adores me, actually, although not fervent about living here. Boresville is what she calls it. As a grand-daughter of Augustus and a princess royal she is accustomed to moving among people less leaden than Jerusalem society. She is shy and withdrawn, which some foolish people mistake for lack of experience; and her delicacy and good manners are lost on most of the people she is obliged to tolerate. She deserves better.

Both of us dream of returning to the Roman circuit, if it is safe. Both of us long to leave behind us the useless burden of trying to understand a people who will always hate us, no matter what kindnesses we show them or concessions we grant them.

Our dreams were interrupted early this morning when the officer of the watch hammered our bedroom door and shouted: "Procurator, we have a mob at the gate!"

Beat that for a morning alarm!

I could hear Claudia mumbling something from her separate bed as I started dressing. She looked only half awake, still absorbed in the aftermath of her dreams. She eased herself up to a sitting position, started rubbing her eyes, then stared around the room as if to check she was in familiar territory.

"I've just woken up from a terrible dream." she said. "It was really weird. I found myself in this..."

"I've just woken into one," I interrupted. "We have a mob at the gate, Claudia. Can't you hear them? Your nightmare will have to wait."

One of the few luxuries Claudia enjoys is recounting her dreams to me. It has become something of a ritual. But this morning her timing was wrong. Having been cheated by a mob that otherwise didn't appear to bother her, she fell back on her bed, closed her eyes and turned to face the wall.

I could hear footsteps advance along the corridor and stop outside the door. Leaving Claudia to her dreams, I went out to face a worried centurion. The Sanhedrin, he explained, had brought a Jewish prisoner for immediate trial. A crowd had gathered. They were beginning to grow restless. Guards had been posted. What were my instructions?

"Don't worry, Marcus", I said. "There will be no

trouble. None of them will dare cross the gateway. It's Passover, remember. According to their religious sensibility, they would become unclean if they entered the fortress."

Marcus looked unimpressed. For him, liturgical niceties did not make for reliable defence strategy.

He is right, I thought, as I crossed the pavement to the gateway where the leaders were plotting the death of one of their own people. Religious sensibility, my ass!

At my approach, the crowd quietened and became still. I looked around at the legion of faces ranged against me, and for a moment I was reminded of a similar crowd that had surrounded my headquarters at Caesarea. But this crowd had come here to beg, not protest. They needed my help, my authority, my permission.

The delegation from the Sanhedrin was headed by a chief priest, Jonathan, son of Annas. He is familiar to me, not least for his hatred of Caiaphas. The courtesies over, Jonathan explained to me that the Sanhedrin had convened and found Jesus of Nazareth guilty of the capital charge of treason; since only I had the authority to execute the sentence, Jesus had been brought to me for judgement.

The appeal to my authority amused me. When people appeal to your authority you can be certain that what they are asking is unimportant. (When it is important, they make up their own minds and worry about appeasing authority later.) The Jews have no problem stoning their religious deviants to death, so their sudden nervousness about execution did not ring true. No, the Sanhedrin needed me to protect their reputation with the people. They needed a Roman execution.

I looked at the prisoner, held between two of the Temple police. I was already familiar with his case, with his daft and dangerous claims, with his curious influence,

174

with his anarchic gift for alienating people from civil and religious authority. All this had already been reported to me by my intelligence sources, including details of the recent parade into Jerusalem that proclaimed him king. I had already decided that the Nazarene had to die. Rome has never tolerated messiahs, nor would it tolerate governors who gave them licence to flourish. The fate of the Nazarene had already been decided by history. The Sejanus factor had confirmed me in this decision.

However, I did not want my soldiers to arrest Jesus. I know how perverse the Jerusalem crowd can be: if I had Jesus arrested, the Sanhedrin might protest to Rome that I was interfering again in religious affairs. Given a choice of victims, a Roman governor or a Jewish messiah, who knows which the Sanhedrin would go for? No, the Sanhedrin would do my work for me: they would make the first move and condemn Jesus publicly. My plan was working well. They were at my gate begging me to do what I was going to do anyway. It would be my privilege to be perverse; I would argue the prisoner's innocence, for a while.

I called the prisoner forward. The Temple police released their grip. Jesus rubbed his upper arms where he had been held, then stepped into the gateway. I led him across the pavement, past the judgement seat, through standing rows of guards, into the praetorium. Neither of us spoke. None of the crowd followed.

In the course of my interrogation the prisoner emerged as an unimpressive individual; but revolutionaries, like comedians, always seem impotent without an adoring crowd to fund their efforts. His responses to my questions were spare and enigmatic. I soon realised that I was not important to him. However, I kept talking.

"There is nothing personal about this," I said. "We

Romans have no interest in your sad religion, in your obsession with the past, in the God who has persecuted you throughout your history, in your turgid quarrelling. As far as we are concerned, you can worship whom you like, organise rituals how you please, invent as many laws as you need or want, chronicle your disasters and then call them scripture. All that is your business. But we have our business, too. We have no authority over what you think or feel, only over what you say and how you behave in public. I know you have no allegiance to Caesar. That doesn't concern me as long as our right to rule is neither challenged by the Temple nor contested in the forum. I am responsible to Rome for that, and I will crush anyone who challenges our natural supremacy or incites others to do so."

While I was speaking I wondered if anything was getting through to the prisoner. He seemed too weary to argue his defence, too resigned to fight the inevitable future that had already been mapped out for him. He looked like a man whose whole energy was being absorbed in keeping his eyes open.

"The charge against you could not be more serious, yet you appear untroubled by its implications. Your Great Council has found you guilty of treason for claiming to be the messiah. Are you the king of the Jews?"

"What do you think?" he asked wearily.

"Look here," I said. "Am I a Jew? Your own people and your own chief priests have handed you over to me. I have brought no charges against you. I did not bring you to this place of judgement. I am only trying to establish the truth."

"What is the truth?" he asked.

"What do you think?" I asked wearily.

The nearer you get to people, I thought, the more incomprehensible they become.

Jesus offered no reply. None was expected. Neither of us was looking to the other for anything. Each of us was driven by his own demons or gods, and nothing either of us said would change that.

I led the prisoner back out to the waiting crowd. On the way, I decided not to make it too easy for the Sanhedrin. When I reached the gateway I announced that I could find no case against Jesus of Nazareth.

My judgement had the desired effect: it stunned the crowd into silence and disbelief. The Roman procurator, arch-enemy of the people, was defending a Galilean peasant against charges of treason! (Some day, I believe, disinformation will become an art form.)

As I looked at the angry faces which stared back at me, I could feel the force of the crowd's speechless torment. Then a feeling came from nowhere, crazy but strangely real, that all the faces in the crowd had merged into one vast pockmarked face which was trying to squeeze itself into the arch of the gateway. Whatever individuality people had, whatever sensitivities distinguished them, one from another, seemed brutally suppressed in this violent image. I felt myself shudder.

To distract myself, I turned and looked at the prisoner. Jesus was standing a couple of paces behind me, to my left, between two guards. If he was beginning to hope for freedom, he showed no signs of it. His head was bowed, his eyes closed, his lips sealed into a narrow line of endurance. He stood like a condemned man patiently awaiting the end of all distractions. He had seen too much and heard too much and felt too much, and in the end benefitted too little from life, to believe in miraculous escapes.

A movement in red caught my eye. It came from one of the high-arched windows above the main door of the praetorium. I could see Claudia stepping out onto a small balcony which was still in shadow. Beneath her feet a row of stone lions stared down at the courtyard. She started signalling something with her right hand, scrawling some letter or figure in the air. I felt embarrassed and turned away quickly, hoping no one had noticed her.

I turned back to face the chief priests and the crowd. I was relieved to see different faces again.

Everything remained strangely quiet. Nothing moved. It was as if the rest of the city had stopped, shocked into stillness by some undefined fear. Yet business was going on as usual. Had to be. I could feel the breath of the morning breeze on my face. From behind me the canopy over the judgement seat stirred, then began to flap in a sudden gust of wind.

My soldiers are not a good audience for silence. They get nervous. They want to do something, make noise, prove why they wear uniforms. The centurion on my right, a man who will fell people as naturally as clearing his throat, looked at the guards stationed around the courtyard, scanned the archers positioned on the battlements, then looked to me for orders.

I confess I was growing uneasy. Did the crowd's silence mean they were resigning themselves to my judgement? Had I misread their intentions so badly? Why did they not protest? Why were the chief priests waiting me out? I had to do something, otherwise my prisoner might walk out of the fortress a free man. And if I lost him, my career, such as it was, would be finished.

One thing I could do, I thought. I could play the release game. Every Passover, the procurator releases a prisoner for the people, anyone they choose. I knew I could use this to my advantage if I could limit them in a choice between a popular Zealot and Jesus of Nazareth. The crowd would be certain to misunderstand what I was proposing.

I cleared my throat. "People of Jerusalem, hear me," I called. "You know the customary Passover amnesty, when we choose to forget the crimes of one prisoner and release him at your behest. Honouring this custom may solve our differences. Whom do you want me to release, Jesus Barabbas or Jesus who is called the messiah?"

The crowd stopped staring at me, stopped holding their breath. People turned to each other as if waking from a dream. Relief was tangible. Smiles were appearing on faces. Expressions became individual again. Voices began to rise and fall in waves of exchange and excitement. Clamour was back. The traffic was moving again.

Curiously, however, the noise around the gateway intensified rather than filled the silence of the courtyard. It was as if the gateway marked the boundary between two incommunicable worlds, rather than the meeting place where two desperate conspirators coupled in the shadows.

I turned and walked over to the judgement seat, which was raised on a covered platform in the middle of the pavement. As I mounted the steps, my bodyguard stood to attention and the officer moved to the right of the chair. I sat down to wait. Meanwhile the prisoner was brought to stand on the left of the platform and ordered to face the chair.

From the direction of the praetorium came the sound of approaching footsteps. I could hear someone, unchallenged, climb the steps of the platform. I was relieved to see my private secretary.

"What do you want?" I asked.

"Governor, your wife sends her respects and begs to see you in private audience."

"Return my respects and tell her I will see her presently, when this business is over."

As I waved him away, I could hear a voice of authority command the crowd to be quiet. Jonathan, son of Annas, stepped forward into the gateway.

"What have you decided?" I asked.

"We would be pleased if your excellency would release Barabbas," he replied.

Behind him the other chief priests shouted, "Give us Barabbas!"

Behind and around them the crowd converted the terrorist's name into a liturgical chant: "Barabbas! Barabbas! Barabbas!"

Hands were clapped, feet were stamped, voices were strained. Startled birds flew up from the towers and battlements, the noise of their flutter sounding like a vast hurrah; they hovered for a few moments between us and the sun, then flew off over the Temple precincts.

So far, so good, I thought. The release of Barabbas was no worry: my soldiers can recapture him any time and waste him at their leisure.

When the crowd had calmed down, I addressed the group of chief priests: "Your choice surprises me, even saddens me, but I have no choice but to honour it. Barabbas will be released. You have my word. But what am I to do with Jesus of Nazareth?"

Silence.

Not another large silence, I hoped, not another still life. I prayed to the gods my plan would work.

A single unidentified voice from the middle of the crowd answered my prayer with the cry, "Crucify him!"

Again I waited for the crowd to calm down. I stood up and raised my hands for silence. "You have made your position clear," I said. "I will give you my judgement shortly. Be patient. In the meantime the prisoner will be scourged."

Before waiting for the crowd's reaction, I turned and left the platform. On the way into the praetorium I explained to Marcus what arrangements to make before my return.

I found Claudia in the bedroom. She was sitting on top of her unmade bed, her knees drawn up, her head leaning forward and her hands clasped around her ankles. She looked like she was examining her toes. When I closed the door behind me, she did not look up.

"Are you all right?" I asked.

"My head hurts," she said.

I picked up two cushions from the floor and put them behind her back. "What did you want to see me about so urgently?"

"About the dream I had," she said.

If my men thought my nervous wife could pull me away from crisis government so she could unravel her dreams, they would laugh me out of the fortress.

"What's the rush about a dream?" I asked, as politely as I could.

"It wasn't a dream like other dreams," she said. "More like an omen." She looked up. "You have to hear it."

I sat down on the edge of the bed. She leaned back against the cushions and composed herself.

"I remember looking into a great hall," she said. "It was vast and beautiful – larger than the Circus Maximus and more ornate than any palace or temple I've ever seen. It was open to the sky and lit by a galaxy of shining stars. Crowds of people were standing around the great hall, men and women and children, all dressed in finery that looked as delicate as a rainbow. They were all looking in the same direction, towards a black marble platform on which stood a golden throne. A man sat on the throne –

their king, I suppose – and he was surrounded by legions of guards and attendants and exotic animals. He was dressed in white linen and a purple cloak lined with gold. I couldn't see his face, for he was wearing the mask of a lamb."

"The mask of a what?" I asked.

"Of a lamb," she said. "I'm just telling you what I saw. In the middle of his hands and feet were huge rubies which sparkled in the brilliant light. His hands rested on the serpent-shaped arms of the throne, his feet on a footstool carved in the shape of a fallen eagle. Above his head, on top of the throne, shone a half circle of light like the rising sun."

"Weird," I said, as I smoothed out a section of the bedclothes.

"There was nothing sinister about what I saw, yet I felt there was so much sadness in the room. Though all the people looked like they belonged there, none of them looked happy."

"Sounds like a meeting of the Royal Society of Noble Melancholics," I said.

Suddenly from outside came the crack of leather hitting flesh. The scourging had begun. Things were under way.

Claudia slid past me to the bottom of the bed, got up, and walked over to the window. With her back towards me, she looked down to the courtyard. For awhile she said nothing. Perhaps she was counting the strokes.

"Is that your dream finished?" I asked.

"No one in the great hall was speaking," she said. "Everyone seemed to be waiting for something to happen. Something did. From behind the throne some trumpeters – I counted seven – advanced in line, bowed to the king, then played three long notes. The great hall started to darken. I saw the stars gradually dim, but the light behind the throne grew brighter. Everyone moved towards the walls, clearing a passage between the throne and the great bronze doors at the end of the hall. For the first time I could see the design of the floor. It was decorated in mosaic with grotesque beast-fighters, except in the very centre, where there was a circle of black and white squares."

From outside I could hear one of my officers bark a command, then the slap of sandals as soldiers ran across the pavement. I began to wonder what was happening outside, in the real world.

"Do you really want to continue with this?" I asked.

Claudia gripped the side of the window. "The two great bronze doors were flung open," she continued. "Nothing was there. Nobody entered, nobody left. They banged shut again. Then the centre of the floor seemed to shudder. Two of the marble squares, one black and one white, opened upwards. Two figures, both naked, slowly emerged from the darkness underneath and stepped into the hall. Their bodies were covered in a fine, pale dust which made them look like premature ghosts. I recognised who they were."

"Who?"

"You and me," she replied. "You and me. The governor and the princess. The people in the great hall stared at us and then slowly turned to face the walls. I remember how their long shadows pointed into the centre of the hall where we stood. The only person to continue facing us was the king. He pushed the footstool to one side and stood up. He lifted his hands to grip the side of his mask. His bodyguards began to strike the marble platform with their long spears. The noise was deafening. The king started to raise the mask from his face."

Claudia broke off. She turned from the window and faced me. She looked ashen, afflicted, strangely vulnerable.

"Then what happened?" I asked.

"That was when I woke up," she said.

"That's it? Pity, another moment and you might have discovered the identity of the king."

"I know the identity of the king. I've seen the face behind the mask."

"But your dream didn't reveal that," I said.

Claudia held out her hand. "Come here," she said. She took my hand. "Look down there. What do you see?"

I looked out the window. "I see the prisoner dressed in purple robes. I see him wearing a crown of thorns. I see his face covered in blood. I see my boys doing their job."

"You are looking at the man behind the mask," she said, her grip tightening on my hand. "It's the prisoner. I'm sure. I know. And I am afraid for us, so afraid for us. You must let him go. Please, I beg you."

"It's only a dream, Claudia, a bad dream." I pulled my hand away. "Besides, it's too late. Things have gone too far. He has gone too far to be saved now. I have to go. We'll talk later."

I left her standing at the window.

I go down to the courtyard and walk across the pavement to the judgement seat. I notice Marcus has done as I ordered: in front of the judgement seat there is a table, and sitting on the table is a large bowl of water.

I look at the prisoner, the pretender king who is about to fall out of his own myth into the reality of death. He is still crowned as his ridiculous title, but he looks more like an unlucky yokel who was drawn into a fight not really his, someone who now wonders why he has a spiked head and a split lip and a shredded back. He has difficulty standing upright. His hands are shaking, his mouth is hanging open, his bottom teeth are red. He gazes out at the world through bloodied eyes, all confidence gone. He looks scared to death.

If this pathetic figure is the messiah, then the God of Israel is still, after all these years, addicted to brutality.

I sit on the judgement seat, under my shield of office, in the shade of the canopy. It is hot now. The sun is blazing. The crowd are waiting, shuffling their feet in the dust. My soldiers are waiting. The prisoner is waiting.

I lean forward and put my hands into the bowl of water. The coolness is comforting. I wash my hands in the face of the crowd. "I am innocent of this man's blood," I declare. "His crucifixion will be your responsibility."

I rise from the judgement seat and walk off the platform. I walk away from the crowd and the cheers and the sponsored hate. I head for the stables. I need a ride outside the city, outside this ring of madness, outside the reach of gods and dreams.

JUDAS
ISCARIOT

Two nights ago I betrayed the only person I have ever loved. Since then, I've been sitting here in this abandoned shepherd's hut, scowling at the dark and wondering how I could have misjudged everything so badly. Particularly Jesus. The whole tragic affair has now gathered its own momentum, and I realise I've set events in motion that will make Jesus a permanent victim of the authorities I have always despised. God alone knows where it will all end. All I know is that I've ended up in this cold dark hideout in the middle of a field I've bought with the thirty pieces of silver. Some bargain I've made!

The wind is up, whining through the cracks in the hut. I'm shivering from the cold. There are no shutters to close against the night, no proof against the storm. The force of this wind seems to penetrate the cracks in my dream; its sound seems to mock my hope that I, Judas, would soon be sitting at Jesus' right hand in a council of war. If ever there was a hope past mending, mine has to be it.

So I find myself alone, once again. I suppose it's true to say that I've been a bit of a loner among Jesus' followers, the odd man out. I am the only apostle not from Galilee, which does nothing to promote a sense of belonging to the others. I was born in Kerioth, a small town in southern Judaea, an accident of birth that was interpreted by the others as a decree of fate. They would say things like, "Of course, Judas, you are different." If that was calculated to excuse me, it failed; it just made me feel foreign to myself. They are all from the northern province, and it's well known that they are a bit simple up there. I'm sure I don't have to draw you a picture. You have your own norths, don't you?

The Galileans have always been a puzzle to me. Geographically, they are cut off from Judaea by the hostile territory of Samaria, and they are surrounded on three sides by Gentile nations. You would think they might catch something of their neighbours' independence of spirit. But you would be wrong. I've never worked out why Galileans are so submissive to foreign domination, why they walk around with the swagger of losers, grinning their obedience to whatever doom is invented for them. They are rightly proud of their beautiful land and lake, but why does their pride take no political form? Why do the Galileans settle for so little? Answer me that. They are a good people, for sure. But you can be too forgiving a victim of aggression, too patient a lover of freedom. You can be too Galilean.

Why did I let myself be fooled into believing that this time the Galileans would be different? The argument of history, which I've spent all day rehearsing, was against my stupid belief.

Look at recent history. After Herod the Great returned from Rome, where he arranged to be proclaimed King of Judaea by decree of the senate, he gathered a troop of mercenaries and marched through Galilee. The peasant farmers and fishermen gave little or no resistance. The Galileans had no leadership, no organised uprising, no guts. By contrast, Herod needed eleven legions and six hundred cavalrymen and five months to retake Jerusalem.

It was the southerners who resisted this arrogant puppet of Rome. It was the southerners who paid the price throughout Herod's pitiless reign of forty years.

When Herod died, Jesus of Nazareth was only an infant. But Herod's memory must have been a fresh wound for any Jew. Control passed to three surviving sons, two in the north, Archelaus in the centre and south. Archelaus inherited his father's ruthlessness but none of his survival skills. After ten cruel years, Archelaus was banished to Gaul on orders from Rome. This left Judaea, Samaria and Idumaea under direct Roman control, through a procurator.

In the same year, Judas the Galilean organised the uprising protesting at the incorporation of Judaea into the Roman province of Syria and the census ordered by Quirinius. Judas was a brilliant man, the founder of the Zealots, whom he led against Roman overlords and Jewish collaborators. Yet the followers of Judas the Galilean are overwhelmingly from the south. Galileans have provided one or two revolutionary leaders, but how many conflicts with Rome have taken place on Galilean territory? Galileans are slow to move from discontent to organised resistance. Before becoming an apostle, Simon the Zealot was one of the few Galileans willing to put his anger to good purpose. He still holds sympathies close to mine. But the rest of the apostles are sleepers, dozy peasants who would allow themselves to be lorded over by the Prince of Devils as long as they could go fishing in peace.

Unlike Judaea, Galilee escaped direct Roman control. It is still ruled by another vicious son of Herod the Great, Antipas, whom Jesus named well as the fox. It was Antipas who became alarmed at the eloquence and drawing power of John the Baptist, which he was afraid could lead to sedition. To prevent a possible uprising, Antipas beheaded John. And John, never forget, was a southerner. Was it any wonder that Antipas thought of killing Jesus because he thought Jesus the Galilean was John the Judaean come back to life? Antipas, as it has turned out, has no reason to fear Jesus or his followers.

So why did I let myself believe that Jesus of Nazareth would transform the Galileans into an organised force for change? Why did I join his luckless movement?

Some people will say that I joined Jesus' group because I had a head for figures and that I betrayed him for the same reason. That is the kind of explanation that might appeal to many: it sounds clever and uncomplicated, it reduces a complex affair to a matter of personal greed. Motive established, accused identified, judgement passed, case closed. Neat and tidy. That way, people are excused the bother of working out my story. They can point the finger at me and feel good about themselves, declaring that they would never betray Jesus for filthy lucre.

Never forget that Jesus invited me to join him. I didn't ask to be an apostle. Jesus approached me and said, "Judas, come and follow me." I was Jesus' choice, no one else's. Soon after I agreed, Jesus invited me to be bursar for the group. He didn't ask Matthew, who had distinguished himself as a tax-collector and, therefore, as a collaborator with the Roman authorities. Tax-collectors are notorious for their creative arithmetic and their fitful loyalties, and Jesus never put temptation in anyone's way. That is why he asked me to be keeper of the purse and look after the little money there was: he knew that I didn't join a band of penniless preachers for the money. He knew I had my own reasons.

Do you think I spent three years with Jesus for the purpose

of buying an arid field with a collapsing shepherd's hut thrown in? Don't fool yourself! I was after bigger stakes than that.

It was through John the Baptist that I met Jesus. Like some of the other apostles, I started out as a disciple of the Baptist. At that time John lived beyond the east bank of the Jordan in the comfortless stony wilderness, so he could avoid the nervous authorities in Jerusalem and Judaea. He started to preach at the busier fords of the river, where people waited for their turn to wade across. Through these revivalist meetings John's reputation spread quickly, and many Judaeans came out to hear him and be baptised by him in the Jordan. I was one of them. And the reason I stayed with John was because he believed that the Messiah was coming soon.

It was the Messiah, John declared, "who will gather his wheat into the barn, but will burn the chaff in a fire that will never go out." I heard that as good news. Our country was run by chaff; I longed to see the chosen one who would burn up this dross of humanity. For this I had been waiting all my life. Every hour of every day I looked forward to another day, the appointed time when the Messiah would lead his faithful people to carry out the sentence of punishment on our enemies. Every day I prayed the great psalm to the God of victories, the cry for the Lord's waiting people to exult in their king;

> Let the praise of God be on their lips
> and a two-edged sword in their hand,
> to deal out vengeance to the nations
> and punishment on all the peoples;
> to bind their kings in chains
> and their nobles in fetters of iron;
> to carry out the sentence pre-ordained:
> this honour is for all his faithful.

That I was one of the faithful, that I wanted this honour of dealing out due punishment, that I was ready with the praise of God on my lips and two-edged sword in my hand, was surely the fruit of my true calling in life. This I believed. My destiny was written in the psalms.

One day, I remember it well, John the Baptist announced: "There stands among you – unknown to you – the one who is coming after me." By this time Jesus had been in our company for some time and had started to baptise with John. None of us knew the identity of the Messiah, but some of us were drawn by Jesus' teaching about the approaching time. Some of us began to wonder about Jesus. Eventually John himself began to wonder about him. Was Jesus the one we had been waiting for?

After John was arrested and thrown into prison, Jesus began his own ministry in Galilee. He chose the twelve of us to join him, symbolic arithmetic without a doubt: one apostle for each of the tribes of Israel. We were up and going. The message was unambiguous: the time for Israel to rise from its sleep had come at last. The alarms had rung.

I began by admiring Jesus and I ended up by believing in him. He was the one we had been waiting for, and I was among the first to recognise this great truth. I came to love the man, you know. I loved the way he picked up the kind of people everyone else had written off, the way he left them with a sense of their own dignity. I admired the way he took on the authorities, face to face, and confronted their posing hypocrisy.

He was gradually setting himself up as the only real alternative to their burdensome leadership: "Come to me all you who labour...learn from me...for my yoke is easy and my burden light."

Things started off slowly, as in all revolutions. At first,

Jesus was regarded as yet another itinerant charismatic, but he has a unique authority in teaching and healing that cannot be easily ignored. Some people were scared of him, the smart people who were sensitive to where his movement could be taken. When momentum gathers, they warned, it will be difficult to cancel the force that emerges from people's frustration and hurt. What will you do, they asked, when people attach their extravagant hopes to your modest venture?

The momentum did gather force, people's expectations did grow, but Jesus cancelled their dreams. It happened after the feeding of the crowd in Galilee, when the Galileans were moved to make Jesus their king. I went crazy trying to contain my excitement. Now we're getting somewhere, I thought. Now is the time. But as the Galileans moved in to make Jesus their king, he ran from them. He ran from them as if he were running from a nightmare future. I stood on the hillside with the Galileans, sharing their bewilderment and hurt as they looked at the disappearing figure of their Messiah. They were showing some political sense and courage, they knew their man, they judged the time was right, they risked their choice publicly. And all they got was a runaway monarch.

How Jesus ran! It was as if his new power were an affliction, his ability to touch people a curse. He reminded me of King Midas, fleeing from his dazzling garden, weeping for innocent hands that would leave the world ungolden and alone.

At first, I couldn't believe what was happening. He is betraying them and their hopes, I thought. If power is access to resources, how could Jesus refuse the help of the Galilean people? Figure that one out, because I am at a loss. When Jesus ran from them, he left behind the only real offer of power he was ever to receive. You don't run away from offers of kingship if you are striving to influence the minds and hearts of people. Anyway, why should the Son of David refuse the kingship that is his by right?

I consoled myself later – for I had to run after him – that the timing must be wrong, not the offer. Perhaps Jesus was biding his time, perhaps he was budgeting his power, perhaps he was waiting for a better opportunity than an offer from a crowd of crazy Galileans to take over the tetrarchy of a fox.

That day in Galilee was frightening not only for me but for the other apostles. Afterwards, we had whispered conversations among ourselves, sharing questions, exchanging doubts about the future, wondering whether we had witnessed a disproof of a new kingdom. Our voices would shrink away when he approached, and when he asked what we'd been talking about, we would look at each other awkwardly, too afraid to tell him.

Sometimes, at night, I used to watch Jesus as he slept and I would wonder what he dreamed about. Did he dream of faraway places, other Galilees, where those who exercised power never maltreated others, never used their authority as a lethal weapon? If he was, he would never wake up in those magical places. Perhaps he dreamt of marrying a secret love and settling for life at normal size, the ordinary round of thrill and boredom and panic. Did he dream of letting go the single-minded compulsion that led him to obscure towns where he scattered words for people who would never thank him? Did he dream words to change people by? Did he dream of someone dreaming him, a power that one day would wake him to a dreamless peace?

Watching him sleeping on the ground, shelterless, my own questions would come to the fore. Had I misjudged

Jesus? Perhaps the sleeping figure wasn't the one we had been waiting for, after all. Would I have to give up the old consolations that the Messiah would look like what they said he would? But that renunciation would be a betrayal of our tradition, stupidly inconsistent with everything Israel had been educated to expect.

I would look at him and wonder: could Jesus mend in me what Jesus had broken in me?

My faith in Jesus was gradually restored over the next few months. Things began to look up. The turning-point was near Caesarea Philippi, a town on the southwest slopes of Mount Hermon. Jesus had been avoiding the domain of Herod Antipas and had led us north from the lake along the Jordan to its sources. One morning he was praying a short distance from us; we were sitting on the ground, grumbling about the length of time we'd wasted hanging around Gentile territory. After his prayer Jesus walked over to us and sat down. Thankfully, he didn't ask what we had been discussing; instead, he had another question:

"Tell me something," he said. "Who do people say I am?"

A risky question, I thought. Who can afford to ask it? The answers we're likely to hear rarely match the answers we hope to hear. All of us mentioned the wild guesses that were doing the rounds, that Jesus was one or another of the great prophets returned to work for our people.

When he heard the recital of names, he didn't look altogether happy. He looked like a man who expected more than a regrouping of the dead to explain his presence. Another question was risked:

"What about you?" he asked. "Who do you say I am?"

There was hardly a pause before Peter answered. He spoke up confidently, as if to make up for all the disappointing guesses. He announced as a fact what we all hoped was true. "You are the Messiah," he said. Like an annunciation it was.

We watched Jesus closely, waiting for him to confirm the truth of Peter's declaration. Around our group at that moment I imagined I could hear the hills listening. Jesus showed no relief, betrayed no recognition. And before we could press him for his own answer, he told us to keep quiet about what had just been said. He didn't deny the title; he was anxious about it. That was enough for me, enough for all of us. That was the nearest Jesus would ever get to acknowledging the truth that was himself.

He quickly changed the subject. It was time, he said, to head south again. He then started to say something about the likelihood of suffering ahead, but I walked away – not because I didn't want to hear him but because I wanted some personal time to savour this truth that Jesus really was the Messiah, however secret. I hugged myself for joy. We were no longer on the run; we were going south, south, south, with the Messiah. We would end up in Jerusalem, triumphant. For sure.

We didn't just end up in Jerusalem, we entered the city in a way designed to shock the authorities. From the time we started to climb the winding road from Jericho to Jerusalem, a journey through heat and haze and dust, Jesus seemed to attract a large following from the throng of pilgrims travelling up to Jerusalem for the Passover feast. The Galileans were prominent among our growing crowd of supporters; they all seemed to know Jesus; some of them were bold enough to express the hope that Jesus wouldn't turn his back on them again, but allow them to honour their reluctant Messiah in the city of destiny.

If Jesus was a secret Messiah, I thought, surely he must

want to slip quietly into the city. No publicity, no fuss, no trouble. But he surprised us all by organising a parade from Bethphage to the city gates. By the time we entered Jerusalem, we had collected a legion of extras: stray dogs, stray children, drunks, anyone who wanted to attach themselves to a loud procession. A carnival it was, with Jesus riding on a donkey and the rest of us screaming our heads off:

Hosanna! Blessings on the Messiah-King,
who comes in the name of the Lord!

I was overjoyed the secret was out, but I couldn't puzzle out why it was let out. If Jesus wanted to keep his Messianic identity a secret, why did he allow so many to proclaim him the anointed King and throw their cloaks on the ground before him? Not only allowed all this, but promoted it. As we descended the Mount of Olives some Pharisees cautioned him about the political overtones of the racket, no doubt believing they were doing him a favour; Jesus, however, showed he was in no mood for controlled enthusiasm. Above the din of the chanting he shouted to his critics that if his followers kept silence the stones would cry out. At this we all stamped our feet in loud approval. The ground shook, almost as if the earth itself vibrated from the force of our recognition.

Everything was out in the open. This was no brief reprieve from the burden of being a confidential Messiah. After that parade, no one could return to the hush-hush of Jesus' mission, least of all Jesus himself. It was as if his destiny had overtaken him and there was no point in trying to silence the shout of truth. At least this time the crowds got his name right.

The next few days found Jesus teaching in the Temple to the crowds of pilgrims. At night our group would retire to the Mount of Olives. All the other apostles noticed with disappointment what I noticed with alarm: something seemed to have happened to Jesus since the jubilant and carefree entry into Jerusalem. His whole manner seemed to change: gone was the openness to the crowd's expectation, gone was the Messianic confidence; instead, he became more reserved, more cautious, more inward, almost melancholic. He was aware the opposition was gathering against him, that spies were measuring every word he spoke, that the authorities would not tolerate him much longer. He knew he was a marked man.

For hours every day he taught the crowds and argued with his critics, but he talked not of the liberation of Jerusalem but of its destruction. At times he was close to weeping, so deeply did he feel with agonising certainty that the future would resign itself to repeat the past.

Jesus seemed to be trapped in a cycle of catastrophic thinking: no matter which way he turned or which topic he discussed, he opened up a horizon of affliction and cosmic disaster. The talk was of famine, war, chaos, confusion, anxiety, fear, violent death. The outlook was anything but liberating. The more I listened to him the less confident I became that he would grasp the opportunity presented to him by the crowds.

After hearing so much disheartening talk, you felt like crawling under a bushel and waiting for the end of the world. Everything was yielding to an inevitable conclusion: Jerusalem was going to take Jesus before Jesus would take Jerusalem.

I was not going to crawl under a bushel. I still held tenaciously to the belief that Jesus was the Messiah; my real anxiety was about his pace. Masterly inactivity was not an option I could reconcile with Messsiahship. Jesus was proceeding too slowly, too hesitantly, too unsurely for a leader. I knew he didn't share my nationalist zeal, but neither did he pronounce any benediction on our oppressors. It was time to free our country from the vicious tramp of the Roman legions. We were already into overtime. And Jesus was the only one mighty in deed and word who had the authority to lead us. That I knew for sure.

In the absence of any plan I felt that I had to do something. I couldn't remain a spectator, watching the sure decline of my master like some ghoulish sightseer at a public execution. My plan was simplicity itself. I would trigger the uprising myself by bringing forward the inevitable arrest of Jesus to the time when the majority of his Galilean supporters were in Jerusalem. The authorities did not need me to arrest Jesus; they had already plotted his capture and were waiting for the opportune moment to move. I was afraid that they would leave it until after the Passover, by which time all the Galilean pilgrims would have left the city.

I decided to take the initiative.

I went to the chief priests, who knew I was one of Jesus' trusted followers, and persuaded them that the opportune time to arrest Jesus was before the Passover. Addressing their fear that Jesus might lead a Galilean uprising when the Roman garrison at Caesarea moved to the city, I argued that Jerusalem would become an arena of bloodshed. No life would be sacred, I told them, least of all their own.

The fools agreed with me, worried as they were about their own safety and the approval of the Romans. The plan was that I would lead the Temple police to where Jesus rested at night, either at Bethany or at the oil press on the Mount of Olives. He was too popular, they explained, to arrest during the day. Yes, I thought, arresting innocents is for the night-shift. I was to identify him in the normal way a disciple greets a rabbi, by kissing him on the hand.

The plan made, they paid me for my trouble. I didn't ask for the money, but I took it readily. It's such a rare pleasure, after all, to get real currency out of priests.

I kept my word. I had to leave Jesus and the other apostles eating the Paschal meal while I went to keep my appointment with the Temple police. I have always hated the police: you get it in your bones and it stays with you for life. I knew they despised me just as I despised them, but they needed me just as I needed them. Ours was a partnership only conspiracy could make.

I led the uniformed thugs down from the Temple mount to the Kidron valley. Judging by the swords and clubs they carried, they were anticipating some resistance. I carried a dagger hidden in my cloak. To avoid attracting attention, we did not light our torches, but the light of the full moon made our passage easy. After descending the slope to the valley, we passed the tombs cut in the cliff, which, in the moonlight, looked like huge outcrops of rock. None of us spoke as we passed through the cemetery.

We came to the Mount of Olives, the place marked by King David's tears when he wept on hearing how he had been betrayed by his trusted adviser Ahithophel. When Ahithophel realised what a blunder he had made, the poor man hanged himself in despair, thus establishing a pathetic record in the scriptures: the only person to commit suicide outside the battlefield. For a moment I looked back at the tomb of Absalom and I wondered where Ahithophel was buried, whether his final mistake had ever been marked as a place for regret and grieving.

We moved up the slope to the Garden of Gethsemane. I could see that most of the apostles were asleep, while a short distance away Jesus seemed to be arguing with Peter, James and John. Looking at them there in the moonlight, asleep or arguing, my heart sank. Not an alert body of men primed for revolution. I started to pray that they would grasp this opportunity and fight for what they believed in.

I went up to Jesus, took his hand and kissed it. "Rabbi," I said.

Jesus looked at me. "Ah, Judas, Judas," he said. He looked beyond me and kept repeating my name, as if he were investing it with the disappointment of a lifetime.

Torches had been lit. Peter shouted to the sleeping apostles, who woke into their worst dream. The guards moved in. When Simon the Zealot realised what was happening, he grabbed his sword and made a casualty of the official nearest him, the high priest's servant. The other apostles started to draw their swords. I drew my dagger from its sheath. We were together. The hour had come.

Suddenly Jesus shouted at us, "Leave off! That will do!"

When the guards took hold of Jesus, the apostles dropped their swords and ran away. Besides myself, only one of them stayed: his name will go unrecorded here, to save his embarrassment. He had nothing on but a linen cloth, and when two guards grabbed hold of him, he left the cloth in their hands and ran away naked. The last I saw of my fellow apostles was a bare bum running into the dark.

I was furious. The apostles who had left everything to follow Jesus were now willing to leave everything to get away from him. I did not move. I could not move. Jesus let himself be arrested as if it were meant to happen. The police dragged him off, leaving me and my revolution behind them.

It all happened so quickly. So very quickly it was all over.

I threw my dagger beside the fallen swords. Our future lay in a heap. I sat down on the Mount of Olives and wept, not so much for the loss of a dream – though the loss was enormous – as for my own foolishness in believing that Jesus was the Messiah who would stand up to the world. That hope had been given the kiss of death.

Before Gethsemane, I saw my betrayal as a constructive act of belief, a tribute to Jesus' capacity to overcome the larger betrayal of our leaders and chief priests, a scream against being tirelessly polite to those who occupy our land as if they were God's appointed merchants.

I believed that Jesus was God's appointed one, the Messiah we had waited for with such an investment of hope. I believed further that God would lean down from his firmament and change the fixed pattern of oppression that has afflicted our people, that God would indeed grant his chosen one as many legions as it would take to rid the promised land of its strutting colonising pagans.

The alternative was to believe that God had left us all to rot. And that would be the ultimate betrayal. That would mean that we just carry on with business as usual, organising empty rituals and mouthing pious platitudes to cheat those who look to us to support their hope, while all the time we nurse our disaffection and hoard our disbelief. That would be a living death.

True disciples are a subversive lot who move between declared loyalty and secret questioning, aware that they can never eradicate in themselves the hope that first attached them to a cause, even when the purpose of their mad pursuit appears more and more futile. Perhaps that is the kind of folly Jesus talked about. I don't know.

As I sit here trying to account for the whole mess, I wonder if the true disciples of Jesus have all abandoned him. Perhaps their own fear and frustration have, at last, come out into the open. I don't say this with any delight; I say it out of concern, a care that seeks to understand the betrayal of disappointment that gives us so many motives to look elsewhere for hope and help. Can you prosecute a disciple for being disappointed or for being a frustrated dreamer? Who can be saved?

If the story of Jesus is ever written, no doubt I will go down in history as the classic traitor. Perhaps I am, but I never betrayed the ultimate cause I believed in. I am sorry for what I have done in a way that you, my friend, can never ever know. You can betray only what you have loved. I still love Jesus. In all my time with him I betrayed him once. Once has been the limit of my defection.

Every history will have its own secret arithmetic.

All I can do now is to pray, to lament, to find a language for my loss and pain in the psalms. This is my prayer:

> Lord, my God, I call for help by day;
> I cry at night before you.
> Let my prayer come into your presence.
> O turn your ear to my cry.
>
> For my soul is filled with evils;
> my life is on the brink of the grave.
> I am reckoned as one in the tomb:
> I have reached the end of my strength.
>
> You have taken away my friends
> and made me hateful in their sight.
> Your anger weighs down upon me;
> my eyes are sunken with grief.

Will your love, Lord, be told in the grave
or your faithfulness among the dead?
Will your wonders be known in the dark
or your justice in the land of oblivion?

As for me, Lord, I call to you for help:
to you I stretch out my hands.
Lord, why do you reject me?
Why do you hide your face?

Wretched, close to death from my youth,
I have borne your trials; I am numb.
Your fury has swept down upon me;
your terrors have utterly destroyed me.

They surround me all the day like a flood,
they assail me all together.
Friend and neighbour you have taken away:
my one companion is darkness.

Everything is quiet now. I am finished praying. The storm has spent itself, the wind has gone somewhere else, everything is holding itself in quietness.

I get up and walk out of the hut. The clouds brood over everything. Perfect stillness, nothing stirring. The rain seems to have seeped away. I walk a few steps and look around. It looks peaceful, the kind of peace you only notice when you can't sleep.

I look up at the sky, searching through gaps in the clouds for some sign, some crazy hope; but all I can see is black distance, intense blackness without measure.

If only I could disappear into that inviting darkness, leave behind the turmoil and the failure and the let down, and the vast grief that seems to cover everything.

Who will remember us? Who will stay up sleepless,

puzzling over the choices we ended up making? Will anyone bother? Will anyone make an effort to credit us with purpose for doing the things we did, even though we read it all so badly?

Who can be saved?

THE GOOD THIEF

My wife's voice comes back to me in all its pain:

"For the love of God, Jarib, will you stay still for a moment and listen to me? Because if you don't listen to me now, you'll end up having to listen to the Romans when they sentence you to crucifixion. You're heading for the rocks of Golgotha. And Golgotha is no place to wise up. If you carry on the way you're doing, stealing people's money, you'll finish your life feeding the birds from a perch on a cross.

"I don't understand you at all. Is being crucified your secret ambition or something? Crosses are for losers, Jarib, for losers. Is that what you want? Do you really want to end up as live-bait for the vultures? Because that, believe me, is what will happen if you don't stop thieving.

"Oh you can smile your charming smile, but you have me demented with worry. I lie awake at night waiting for the guards to smash in the door and drag you from our bed, leaving me and the kids to scream at your absence. And when I do manage some sleep, I dream I'm standing on Golgotha at the foot of your cross, looking up at the body I know and love, while everyone else stares at a common thief, mocking your useless pain. Then when they go home to play happy families and share their safe disgust of you, I get to come back here, to a fatherless house and to kids who look to *me* to account for what's gone wrong.

"But you know what? I can explain nothing, Jarib, nothing, nothing, nothing. I'm all out of explanations.

"That is one hell of a dream for the future, a hell of a dream. How can I get it into your skull that you are throwing away *our* future? We're tied to each other, for better or worse. Your future is not your own. Each day, each hour, I live watching you die, wasting your life. You'll end up as part of the weekday litter of the Romans. That will be your future. What will be ours?

"Do you want to leave me and the kids to spend the rest of our lives howling at your stupid memory? We love you, Jarib, you must know that. I need a husband, they need a father, and all we get is a thief who spends his energy between stealing and running away. What the hell are you stealing *for?* It's not for us. Tell me. Go on, explain it to me. Explain it to the kids. Tell them how it will be when they have no clothes on their backs and no food in their mouths because their father could never be satisfied with enough. Tell us, damn you!"

I did not answer Miriam then. It is too late to answer her now. I have caught up with her nightmare. I am high up on the rocks of Golgotha, roped to a cross. Higher up, the vultures creak with impatience. It is too late now for everything. All that is left is pain and nothing.

Her words are lacerating the inside of my head, hurting me more than the lashes on my back or the shrieking bones in my arms. I love her and the children, even though I know my love is worthless.

How could I have told Miriam that I had a passion which ruled my love for her? How could I have explained my obsessive love for the freedom of my country, which made me steal money? When I went around with the tax-collectors, protecting them from bandits, I exacted what money I could from people. I sent it to the Sicarian rebels, the dagger-men. Judas Iscariot is one of them, I'm sure, and I expected someone like him to be strung up here beside me. Not Jesus.

I risked my life for a cause that has dominated my life. I knew that sooner or later the Romans would catch up with me. Now I hang here paying the price. I can bear it. What I cannot bear is that I've condemned Miriam to pay a terrible price. Every cause and every truth has its innocent victims. I have sentenced my wife and children to spend the rest of their lives as victims of my cause.

I know why I am here. God alone knows why Jesus is here, unless innocence has become a capital offence. I'll probably last three or four days, but I doubt if Jesus will last another hour.

The Romans have given him the kind of savage attention that goes beyond the call of duty. I watched them prodding him up the rocks – he wasn't able to carry the cross-beam because his shoulders were raw and his feet kept giving way under him. The soldiers kept tripping him up, then loudly apologising. When he staggered up here, the waiting women offered him a drink. In their midst, I could see Miriam. I could feel her love and her sense of defeat as she watched Jesus. He brought the drink to his lips and then turned away, as if impatient for everything to be over.

Around his neck was a wooden tablet inscribed with the charge against him. The soldiers pulled this off, stripped him, then tripped him over a rock onto the ground. They nailed his hands to the cross-beam. In the middle of the beam, they nailed the charge against him, "This is Jesus, the King of the Jews."

Some scribes moved forward and objected to the wording on the tablet. Two of the soldiers unsheathed their swords. The scribes retreated. The soldiers laughed.

An officer stood surveying the wooden uprights implanted in the rocky ground. His eyes came to rest on the tallest stake, which stands between my cross and the cross of another convicted robber. He pointed to it and shouted to the execution squad, "Put him up there, between those two prize imbeciles! Where he belongs!" He looked around at the bystanders as if expecting some trouble. There was none.

The soldiers promptly obeyed the order. One of them picked up the scaling-ladder which was lying at the foot of my cross, placed it against the back of the stake, climbed it and waited. Four soldiers lifted the cross-beam, two on either side, and dragged Jesus the short distance. They lifted the beam above their heads, then the soldier on the ladder gripped it with both hands and raised it slowly into the groove on top of the stake. When he did this, almost without effort, the others cheered him for his knack. He shook a fist in the air to acknowledge their recognition. He was pleased with himself. While he secured the beam in place the tallest of the soldiers sat Jesus on the peg that was fixed to the middle of the upright. That done, he held Jesus' feet while they were nailed to the rough bark.

Miriam turned away, covering her ears with her hands.

When Jesus' body was fixed in place, the soldiers stood back to admire their handiwork. They nodded to each other and turned away.

People come and stare at us. They look around, they look up, they look around again, inspecting the details of grief. They point, they whisper to each other, they shake their heads, and they go on their way. We are part of the Passover spectacle, an optional side-show for pilgrims. Just another city sight of those caught suffering.

Suddenly a small boy breaks away from his mother. Everyone can hear her Galilean shout, "Mark, come back here!" The boy runs up to the foot of Jesus' cross. Staring up at the figure of Jesus, he takes in the punishing clarity of everything. He looks stunned, rooted to the spot. His mouth is open, his arms are tight by his side, his fists clenched. Some of the onlookers murmur disapproval, ill at ease with this child seeing too much.

The boy starts unclenching his fists slowly, as if he is letting go of some awful affliction. He reaches out his right hand, like a blind child groping for sense, and touches the feet of Jesus.

"Mark!" his mother shouts.

The boy doesn't appear to hear her. He continues to stare up at Jesus, continues to stroke the feet of Jesus, as if his look or his touch might bring forth some explanation for this naked defeat. Neither the boy nor Jesus says a word.

"Mark!" his mother shouts again.

The boy's eyes stop looking at Jesus, his fingers stop touching the torn feet. For a brief moment he looks at me, and I see his eyes red as wounds. He turns away and starts to walk back. When he has gone only a few steps, he turns his head and looks back as if he has left something behind. His mother comes forward and draws him into herself. I hear her say, "Come away, son, there is nothing you can do." He glances back. She grips his left hand, tugs it, pulls him past the onlookers and back down the road to the city gates.

People come and go. Time passes. The flies are fed. The vultures absorb their territory. The wild dogs stretch in the heat and stare out their rivals.

The soldiers yawn and play dice, waiting for their replacements. From time to time one of them shouts in triumph at his small win.

A cluster of priests and scribes keep their own company, biding their time until the death of Jesus frees them to go.

The women wait. Miriam sits on the rocky ground, her head between her knees, her hands clasped tightly around her ankles. A woman sits beside her and slowly strokes her back.

Above us all the scorching sun beats down from a cloudless sky.

Jesus is quiet. I can hear the rasp of his breathing. Sometimes his body lifts and shudders, then settles back on the wooden peg that takes his weight. His head has dropped forward now, his chin pressing against his chest, his mouth hanging open. He looks as if he is bowed down by the weight of some ancient sadness. I know that the worst of my bodily pain is still to come, but there can be little more to come for Jesus. I pray to God to take him. He looks spent, finished.

Two men arrive and join the huddle of the religious group that stands apart from the rest of the onlookers. Both of them glow with self-importance as they acknowledge the group's fawning greeting and listen to the reports, nodding approval when some line particularly pleases them. The priests and scribes point to Jesus' cross, grinning like schoolboys taking credit for their own handiwork. The two leaders smile. And as if their presence has lent authority to the group, someone shouts out: "Come down from the cross, Chosen One, and show us what you're made of!"

Soon the others take up the chant: "Come down, come down, come down!"

Neither of the leaders joins in. Both looked charmed by what they see and hear. Their indifference to the pain that faces them sickens me more than the cramp that is overtaking my body. From where I hang I envy them their freedom, but I am revolted by the rot from which it stems.

The priests and scribes find an unusual ally in the other criminal, who starts up his own abuse: "Aren't you supposed to be the Christ? Prove it! Save yourself, and save us when you're at it!"

I tell him to shut up. Then I take a deep breath and scream at them all: "Jesus has done nothing wrong! He is innocent as you are guilty!"

Some vultures fly off from the stakes nearby. The soldiers pause in their game and glance over at the officer of the watch. Everything goes quiet. Miriam looks up at me, horrified. I know she is worried the officer will give the order to break my legs. She keeps looking at me, begging me with her eyes to keep quiet.

I turn to look at Jesus. He manages to lift his head and turn towards me. My heart goes out to him. I say to him, "Jesus, remember me when you come into your kingdom."

He goes into himself to gather what resources he has left. He struggles out his reply: "Today, Jarib, you will be with me in paradise."

Suddenly his body lifts to grasp the air for help, and through his pain he cries out: "Abba, into your hands I entrust my spirit. Abbaaaa..."

The last cry of "Abba" lingers in the stillness, like an

echo of some spent force. The effort takes everything out of him. His body no longer finds the peg to rest on but lurches forward, hanging on the nails.

Jesus of Nazareth is dead.

The officer shouts a command. The soldiers move in.

MARY, THE WIFE OF CLEOPAS

Everyone seems to be leaving Jerusalem. The city is emptying as if there's been news of a coming earthquake, but it's only the end of another festival. Passover is over for another year: the lambs have been dutifully slaughtered, the blood smeared on the doorposts, the meal shared as a memorial of the exodus. Having eaten the memory of ancient liberation, the pilgrims head for ordinary life again. The gates of the city are crowded with the press of people eager to get back to whatever they left behind them.

Whether my husband Cleopas or myself will ever get back to ordinary life again is doubtful. Passover, for us, has been a deadly affair, a time of unutterable misery. Everything that could go wrong has gone wrong. Our beloved master, Jesus of Nazareth, is dead. And he didn't die peacefully in his bed; he was put to death, in the most cruel and humiliating fashion, by the authorities we have been educated to respect. Their Passover menu was lethal: slaughtered lamb, spilt blood, served up to kill a new memory.

As the two of us take the road to Emmaus we are heartsore from grief, from the senselessness of it all. Looking at Cleopas I think my heart will break: he looks like a man who has lost everything in life but the breath in his body. It's as if his loss has scaled away everything I've known of him, stripped him of his appetite for life and his easy good humour, revealing not the man I know and love but a disconsolate angel with nothing to say and nowhere to go but away from a once heavenly city.

He has no tears left in him.

Early this morning, after some women from our group went to the tomb and did not find the body of Jesus, they came back saying they had seen a vision of angels, who declared he was alive. I was excited by the news; Cleopas was cautious. I wanted to run to the tomb but Cleopas caught my hand and told me to wait. He was afraid of being cheated by some mad hope; he wanted, he said, to protect me from running to nothing. Nevertheless, we waited for the runners to return. They said the tomb was empty, but there was nothing to be seen of Jesus. Cleopas nodded, took my hand, pulled me away from yet another disappointment, and headed for the city gates.

The road we're taking to Emmaus, which winds through Gabaon and Beth-horon, is quiet. We have left the crush of pilgrims behind us, most of whom will be heading north. It is hot. Even the morning sun seems to miss nothing under its merciless clarity, blistering everything around us. The geography is comfortless. All around us is barren and stony and gray. We live in a land of too much light, too many rocks, too much zeal. There is no shade or shadow or nuance. For the first time I think of the landscape as menacing: I see it as hard, upright, unyielding, defiant, mute, even violent. And this is the landscape that wastes so much masculine energy, leads to so much earnest fighting about territory that is always called religious, and inspires such an endless massacre of innocents. The prizes seem so paltry, I think, as I look around. Who ends up claiming the most historic rubble? Who gets emotional, in the first place, I wonder, about a land that has lived with its own abstinence for so long that it is indistinguishable from a vast stony graveyard?

This is a womanless landscape, yes. Or is this just my hurt talking?

Is it any wonder I loved Jesus so much? His very difference made him religious. He spoke to us of God through living water, wheat fields, vineyards, fruit trees, flowers, fish, bread and wine. He greened our landscape with virtue; he humanized it with stories of ordinary people. His victories were of love, trust, forgiveness, tenderness, forbearance. If you're a woman you get a wee bit tired listening to talk about the grandeur of the wilderness and the glory of the battlefield and the majesty of the mountain, as if these are the only places you can meet God. You want God in the kitchen, in the miracle of daily bread, in the majesty of everyday love, in the grandeur of your sleeping child's face. Jesus gave us all this. Little wonder he said his kingdom was not of this world.

But Jesus is dead now. Dead, dead, dead. And the best in us has died with him.

Some distance ahead of us, through the haze, I can see a caravan of travellers turn off the road, no doubt to take a short-cut through the hills. I wonder, uselessly, if their lives have been renewed or destroyed by the Passover.

"What will become of us now?" I ask Cleopas. Up to now he has said nothing, probably because he thinks there is nothing to say; but I just want to hear him speak, say something, anything.

He draws in a breath, hunches his shoulders, and breathes out loudly as if trying to expel some of the hopelessness within. I can see the sweat on his forehead and above his upper lip.

"Cleopas?"

"I heard you, Mary," he says. "I heard you." His voice seems to come to me from a great distance. "I wish there was something I could say to cheer you."

He stops and touches my arm. I want so much to embrace him, but I'm afraid we'll end up crying again.

"We'll go home and try to stay alive," he says. "It's not much, I know, but together we'll try to pick up the pieces. Maybe we can get back to how it was before we met him."

"I doubt that," I say as gently as I can. "We can't pretend nothing has happened. We're different people."

"I know," he says as he turns and starts walking again. "But it's difficult to accept what's happened, just as it's difficult to know who to believe in any more. What has Passover made us? We're now ex-disciples of a dead prophet. Look at us: two refugees escaping from a city where everything we hoped for collapsed before our eyes."

I'm thinking of something to say in reply to Cleopas, for I'm afraid we might lapse into another long silence, when I become aware of someone close behind us. When I turn my head to look, I see a man striding towards us, his head uncovered, his long arms swinging by his side. He looks like a man in a hurry to be somewhere, someone who has to make up for lost time; but when he gets level with us, he slows down and falls into step beside us.

"Peace," he says, nodding to each of us in turn.

"Peace," we murmur back.

Cleopas eyes the stranger closely and then glances over at me. I can read his tired look: what have we done to deserve this?

We don't want to be rude to the stranger, but neither of us is in the mood for polite diversions. Then, as if we've previously agreed what to do in awkward moments like this, we both slacken our pace to a dawdle, to allow our unwanted travelling companion to move on and leave us in peace. But he slows down, too, and keeps walking by our side.

"What are you discussing as you walk along?" the stranger asks amiably, as if we've been discussing the weather.

At the question, our dawdle is reduced to a standstill. I look at Cleopas, whose downcast face must match my own. For a long moment I think he might ignore the question, excuse us and walk on. There is pain written all over his face. He looks down at his feet as he shifts them back and forth in the dust, then he looks up at me; but I have no help left in me. I feel useless.

He clears his throat. He has his own question for the stranger: "Are you the only visitor to Jerusalem who doesn't know the things that have been happening there these last few days?"

"What things?" the stranger asks.

This new question prompts Cleopas to start walking again. This is like a bad dream, I think. How can this man be so ignorant of the trial and execution of Jesus? After all, what happened to Jesus wasn't exactly a secret affair. Or is this man one of nature's dangerous innocents, the kind of person who blithely goes through life, untouched by the offence of other people's suffering? Looking at him, I feel my questions are unfair. What would Jesus do, I ask myself, if he were faced with this inquisitive man?

"It's difficult to know where to start," I say to him. "We are followers of Jesus of Nazareth."

"Were," corrects Cleopas.

"You must have heard about Jesus," I continue. "There was no one like him, no one. He proved he was prophet mighty in work and word before God and all the people.

He was close to God, so very close. Anyone with eyes could see the goodness that was in him and the power that came out from him. We knew him, you see, and we loved him with all our hearts. That is why we became his disciples."

The stranger nods his head, but I sense he is not going to speak. This question-master who stole up on us so quietly seems in no rush to ask any more questions. His face is polite, withholding.

"Then it all came to an end," Cleopas says, aggrieved and suddenly alert. "And us with it. I find it difficult enough to understand why so many people turned against Jesus but I'll never be able to make out why our chief priests and leaders rejected him so finally and with such violence. Aren't they supposed to be God's spokesmen? It was sinful what they put him through, handing him over to be sentenced to death, then having him crucified as if he were a common thief. And another thing I can't work out is this: if God's hand is in everything, where was God in all this? We were there, but where was God when Jesus was dying on Golgotha?"

He hesitates, less sure of himself, and wipes the sweat from his forehead with the sleeve of his tunic. "Forgive me, I'm confused," he goes on. "I don't mean to question the ways of the Almighty, but if God can send an angel to save Isaac from being slaughtered, why couldn't he do the same for Jesus? Why didn't the angel come?"

Cleopas asks the last question with such passion that it sounds like a cry for help. He looks up at the dazzling blue sky as if he might find some answer scribbled there, or might yet be surprised by some unpunctual angel come to undo the mistake of suffering. Whatever he is looking for, there are no answers forthcoming either from me or the reticent stranger.

For a little while we journey on in silence, left to listen to our own thoughts and the rhythm of our steps. Ahead of us the road unscrolls its way to a shifting but unvaried horizon of hills and stones and dust. I wonder if we'll ever get to the finishing line. A few trees, mostly acacia or jujube, do their best to soften the harsh landscape, but their bravado seems to highlight a larger loss. Above us the sun is as it always is, vast and overriding and relentless.

This road, this heat, this journey, this stranger, this silence. Is it only a matter of time, I wonder, before everything in life becomes a question?

Just a week ago Cleopas and I were on another journey, from Bethphage to Jerusalem, accompanying Jesus on his entry into the city. A week ago we didn't notice the heat or the stones or the dust: everything was a joy to us, so delighted were we to hear our hopes proclaimed in the cry "Hosanna! Blessings on the Messiah-King who comes in the name of the Lord!" A week ago. Since then, everything held by hope has faded into memory.

"We had a hope," I find myself saying to the stranger. "Not just Cleopas and me, but the whole crowd of us who followed Jesus. We all hoped that he would be the one to set Israel free. We could see he was a prophet, as I said, a great prophet like Moses, but the important thing is that what we saw led us to expect more. Cleopas was always saying 'Mark my words, Jesus is more than meets the eye.'"

"Sure I was," Cleopas says. "And I meant it at the time."

"Of course you did," I say. I turn to our companion again. "I don't know if you know what I mean, but Jesus was the kind of person who attracted your hope. Somehow, I don't know how, our hope seemed secure with him, well placed, like a sure bet. Everything he did and said seemed to confirm that. He became everything we hoped for, and more. When we looked at him we saw our hope fulfilled."

"And that's the problem," Cleopas protests, his voice unnaturally loud, his hands held out in front of him as if they hold the weight of what he's saying. "That's the sadness of it all. We burdened Jesus with too much hope. We forgot that our grand expectations could be brought down by so many other things in life."

His voice quietens and he returns his hands to his sides. He says, "Sometimes, without knowing it, you let your hope run too far ahead of you, as if hope can manage by itself in the real world. You hope that everything you cherish will endure, that time will secure what your heart yearns for, that men's evil designs will never destroy your belief in human goodness, that God will not abandon what his love has created. And then it all proves too much when your hope becomes a fatal casualty of what actually happens. That's our story. Our hope ended up being hammered to death on the cross. How can we hang onto our hope in Jesus as the Messiah when he is well and truly dead? Our hope in him can never be reclaimed, for death finishes everything, empty tomb or no empty tomb."

I don't know about the stranger, but I don't understand everything Cleopas says; I do, however, more than I can say, feel his pain and disappointment.

His last remark about the empty tomb can make no sense to the stranger, so I try to explain: "This morning some women from our group went to anoint the body of Jesus, but when they got there they found the tomb empty. They ran back and told us they had seen a vision of angels, who declared he was alive. When some of our friends went to check the story, they saw the empty tomb but nothing of Jesus."

Then, as if he can no longer contain himself, the

stranger exclaims, "How foolish you are! So slow of heart to believe in all the prophets have said! Was it not necessary that the Christ should suffer all this before entering his glory?"

Cleopas and I are so stunned by the stranger's inexplicable outburst that we stop in our tracks. I see Cleopas open his mouth to say something, but only a guttural sound emerges; and with his mouth still hanging open, he stares at the stranger as if this man has just shared some disreputable secret.

I feel hurt and confused. We have been opening our hearts to a taciturn pilgrim who now turns out to be our accuser and calls us fools; we have been telling him how Jesus was rejected, and he reproaches us for missing all that the prophets foretold. We have been explaining how our hope in Jesus as the Messiah was cruelly cancelled by his death, and he announces that the suffering of the Messiah was an unavoidable journey to glory.

Were our thoughts as perplexing to the stranger as his are to us?

The stranger starts walking on, and as he goes ahead of us he neither pauses nor looks back. Cleopas and I stand on the dusty road, our heads bowed under the heat of the blazing sun. We linger in this no-man's-land like two lost travellers who don't know which way to turn. We are slow to move, but move we do.

For a few minutes the two of us follow in silence behind the stranger.

Gradually our pace quickens and we catch up with him, and when we return to our former positions, one on either side of him, he starts speaking to us again. His manner is as patient now as his voice is gentle.

"About suffering and rejection," he says, "the prophets were always right: look at how they lived, listen to all they said, remember how they died. The mighty prophet like Moses, the Messiah, could not have avoided the traditional destiny of the prophets if God's plan was to be accomplished. The very thing you say destroyed your hope is what makes for the fulfilment of scripture.

"You feel Jesus' death was an act of desertion because you believe his suffering was avoidable. You wanted a Messiah immune from frustration and pain and death, a regal spectator of other people's suffering, one who would never be anyone's victim, not even God's.

"You believed in a Messiah who could only succeed in his mission by detachment and power and success, never by making himself vulnerable, never by permitting himself to be wounded, never by allowing others to do to him what others do to so many innocents. You burdened yourselves with the wrong hopes.

"Believe me when I tell you that the way of the Messiah is the way of Jesus, the way of long suffering love. Loving God is not a defence against disappointment, neither is it a guarantee of safety; it is a journey through the suffering that cannot be avoided if one is to remain faithful to the word of God. Long-suffering love makes its way with a cross on its back. It takes on its shoulders what so many people are anxious to avoid: responsibility for their hate, their meanness of spirit, their violence, their legion of sins.

"You speak of the passion of Jesus as if it were only something done to Jesus. Jesus was not just submissive, passive, acted upon; he took suffering on himself, he chose to make visible what everyone wants to hide. It was his own passion for life and goodness that led him not to despise its consequences in death. It was his own passion for God and for people that enabled him to make the journey from Gethsemane to Golgotha.

"Better for the Messiah to pass lovingly into the realm of death, for the sake of others, than dwindle into a passionless glory that costs nothing and, therefore, means nothing.

"And you are shocked that his love is rejected. My friends, if only you knew the prophets! Look at their story."

The stranger continues his teaching by appealing to the ancient writings. Beginning with Moses and going through all the prophets, he interprets the passages of scripture that refer to the suffering and death of our beloved Master.

As we journey closer to Emmaus, the teacher does something for Cleopas and me that we could not do for ourselves: he illuminates our own experience of recent events by his deep knowledge of the word of God. Through everything he says he invites us to think again, to look again, to understand anew.

When we come to the turn-off for our village, Cleopas and I naturally turn right into the little track that leads to Emmaus, but the teacher pauses and stays on the road. Without a wave or a word of goodbye, he makes to continue his journey on the way that leads to the Great Sea.

When I see him begin to move away from us, I feel an enormous sadness come over me. It's as though I am watching yet another sign of hope withdraw from us and, without excuse or apology, head elsewhere until it becomes absorbed in some amorphous world, leaving Cleopas and me to return to our makeshift lives.

"Teacher!" Cleopas calls.

The teacher stops and turns around. Cleopas takes my hand and we both walk over to the man we don't want to lose.

"Don't go," Cleopas pleads. "We would like you to stay with us. It is nearly evening and the day is almost over."

"Come home with us," I say. "Please come home with us."

"You would honour our house," Cleopas adds rather shyly, his hand gripping mine more tightly.

Our fellow traveller smiles at us. Looking at him I get the impression he is relieved we have shortened his road. Though I cannot be certain, I think he was hoping we would ask him home. This thought delights me.

"I'll be happy to stay with you," he says.

Cleopas releases his grip on my hand and says to our guest, "Good. Let's go."

For the short time it takes to reach the village, the three of us pick our way down the stony track. Cleopas leads the way; I follow behind him; the teacher brings up the rear. None of us speaks, but I feel the silence is a happy one, expressing a new intimacy.

As the last part of the track curves sharply to the right before entering the village, our three shadows merge into one long indeterminate shape on the ground, making it look like a gawky giant hurrying to keep some rendezvous in Emmaus. I am still smiling at the thought when we reach the door of the house.

Once inside, the house seems mercifully cool compared to the heat we have endured, and the partial darkness is a welcome relief from the brightness outside. Cleopas waits inside the threshold and formally greets the teacher into the house by kissing him on the hand and pouring a little oil on his head. Thus anointed, the teacher is invited to sit on the low bench beside the door. As I set the table with barley bread, olives, fruit, cups and a jug of wine, Cleopas pours water into a dish and goes down on his knees to wash the feet of our guest.

I know that Cleopas, like me, must be wondering whose feet he is washing; but our tradition of courtesy forbids us to ask the name of our guest. It will be for him, if he chooses, to tell us in his own time who he is.

After washing our hands, we take our place at table. Before Cleopas says a word, the teacher takes the bread and says the blessing; then he breaks the bread and hands it to Cleopas and me.

As we take the bread from our mysterious table companion, at this moment appointed by God, our eyes are opened for the first time and we behold the true identity of the stranger. It is Jesus himself, our beloved master!

Cleopas and I look on the radiant face of our risen Lord, the face we believed was lost to us forever, and we are speechless for joy; but no sooner do we recognise him than he vanishes from sight. Suddenly, without warning, there is no one there. Suddenly there are only two of us in the room.

We both rise slowly to our feet and stare at the empty place. Never before have I looked at the shape of an absence, never before have I been so intensely aware of someone's presence.

Instinctively I move over to where the Lord sat and I touch the small wooden seat, but I feel only the rough texture of the wood; I touch the table where he leaned, but it is only a table.

"He is not here; he is risen," Cleopas says softly, echoing this morning's message from the empty tomb.

"Yes," I say, now patting the air like a blind woman confused that she can't touch what she feels is there.

"Mary," Cleopas says.

I start fingering the bread Jesus held out to us. The stranger gave himself away in the breaking of this bread,

I tell myself, the teacher became Lord for us through offering us this food.

"Mary," Cleopas says again.

I let go of the bread. Cleopas and I turn to one another and, without a word, we fall into each other's arms and we hold one another tenderly and for long until our tears stop flowing and our trembling bodies come to rest.

"Oh, Mary," Cleopas says. "Wasn't your heart burning within you as he talked to us on the road and explained the scriptures to us?"

"It still is," I say. "He lit a fire in our hearts and I hope it will never go out again."

"But we must go," Cleopas says, easing himself out of our embrace.

"Where?"

"To Jerusalem," he says.

"When?"

"Now, of course! We must tell the others the good news."

"Of course!" I exclaim.

Without a backward glance, we leave behind the table set for eating, the half-dark of the room, the shelter of our home; we leave behind our tiredness and sorrow and ignorance, and we retrace our steps up the track to the road, where we turn left for Jerusalem.

The sun is lower now and it casts a soft pink light over the landscape as far as the eye can see. A short distance away, on the slopes of the hills, a vast herd of sheep is grazing; and around them, patiently taking up their positions, the shepherds prepare to gather them in for the evening, to the dry stone-wall enclosures.

From somewhere on the hillside comes the plaintive sound of a shepherd's flute, the notes rising and falling in some secret signature-tune to the flock. As Cleopas and

I hurry on our way, the fading music spurs us on and on to a Jerusalem where new stories will be told, where new music will be played, and where a remnant of disciples, made lonely by loss and disappointment, will be gathered into one fold by the undying love of the risen Lord.

PALESTINE UNDER EARLY PROCURATORS

Tetrarchy of Herod Antipas

Tetrarchy of Philip

Under Pontius Pilate

- - - Decapolis

▲ Fortresses

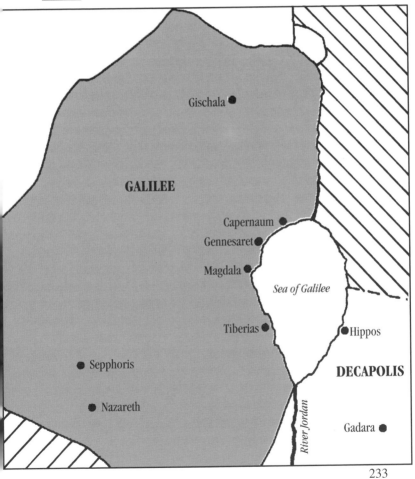